Colourful Threads

A collection of poems woven from the heart

Written by Megan Reda

Colourful Threads - A book of poetry

Copyright © 2024 Megan Reda

All rights reserved. Apart from any use under the Copyright Act 1968, no part may be reproduced by any process without prior written permission from the publisher. You can read or post the poems with references from the Author noted.

Scripture quotations marked THE VOICE are taken from The Voice™.

Copyright © 2008 by Ecclesia Bible Society. Used by permission.

All rights reserved.

ISBN: 978-0-6488386-2-3

Front cover - *Handwoven Textile Heart designed by Megan Reda*
Book cover web layout– *Chris Collard @ ChrisTeena Gifts*
Book cover proofing – *Candice Jade Graphics*
Photography - *Oliver Mehra Photography*
Typesetting - *Faith Anne Kasuku - Upwork*
Printed – *Ingram Spark*
Self-published: *Megan Reda 2024*

Dedicated to

Jesus, my best friend.

Foreword

I felt incredibly privileged when my dear friend Megan invited me to write the foreword for her latest book, "Colourful Threads". Our friendship blossomed in early 2020, and since then God has woven us together as sisters in faith. I am eternally grateful for this precious bond we share.

Shortly after we became acquainted, Megan approached me and asked if I would review the draft of her first book, "My Child and the Tapestry of Life". I was captivated from the very beginning. It serves as a testament to the power of God, showcasing Megans' triumph over numerous challenges and her victorious journey through Jesus Christ. "Colourful Threads" is a collection of divinely inspired poems that Megan has been blessed to share with us, offering hope, encouragement and solace.

These poems have been birthed from her love for Jesus. As you delve into the pages, you will undoubtedly find glimpses of yourself, just as I have.

I pray that these words will draw you into a deeper relationship with Christ, touching your heart in profound ways. They were written just for you.

I know, without a doubt, this is a supernatural book. Megan collected twenty poems over a 30-year journey of salvation and healing. Then, in October 2023, I witnessed an incredible thing. Poetic words started to rain down from heaven every morning into Megan's heart. In a few months, she soon had a collection of over one hundred poems. God poured down His Spirit upon Megan to capture the essence of His heart.

Our lives are like intricate tapestries, woven with vibrant threads, many of which are beautifully depicted in the poems you are about to read. Therefore, I extend an invitation to you today to sit down with the Holy Spirit as He ministers to your soul through these anointed pages.

Business Owner
V.P. Heartweavers Inc.

Jill Ross

Acknowledgements

I wish to thank my family for loving me as unconditionally as you do. My Mother is the epitome of love. The nurture she has surrounded me with can be seen through the threads of my life and many of the poems in this book. I am who I am because of her beautiful grace.

To my three children whom I adore with my whole being. My two sons-in-law and daughter-in-law. My grandchildren. You are all ingrained on my heart.

To my Heart Weaver sisters. Your faithfulness to God and this vision goes above and beyond. Your fierce love for this call and your never-ending generosity, honesty and support to me is a gift from God into my life.

To David and Sonia. Your wisdom, words of encouragement and prayers are a blessing. Your belief in me have always seen the bigger picture and you remind me when I need it the most. I will be forever grateful for you both in my life.

And to those whose threads of life have woven into mine to bring me inspiration to capture life in verse, I say thank you.

Poems found alphabetically

Introduction
A Masterpiece
A New Door
A New Year
A Perfect Life
Always There
Amazing Love
An Ode for the Seer
Atmosphere Changer
Basking in the Goodness of the Lord
Be Still
Brand them Anew
Bullied No More!
Call Them In
Castles on the Sand
Christmas Story
Colourful Threads
Creation
Daughter of the King
David and Goliath
Each Day is New
Encounter
First Love
First Things First
Forgiveness - I did choose
Getting it Right
God is Listening
God is Love
God-blessed Ride!
God-given Gift
God's Glory Train
God's Holy Fear
God's Love for Me
God's Love is Coming

God's Planned Call
Heart Shine Check
Heart Weavers
Hero Unaware
His Love
Honour
Hope
I am a City on a Hill
I am Free!
I will Always Remember
I will get There
I, Jesus will Return!
If you only knew
It's not too Late
Jesus is Calling
Jesus is the Reason
Just Believe
Just say Yes!
Keep Me Anchored
Kingdom RAC
Letting Go
Lord, I'm getting older!
Lord, I'm Listening
Lord, I Pray
Lost Anointing
Love and Unity
Love, Share and Care
Ministry behind the Mask
Money has a Voice
Morning Love Poem
Morning Song
My Bible
My Call
My Child
My Shepherd
My Special Friend
Never Leave or Forsake
No more Lust
No more Mountains

No More Questions
Parents, please
Perfect in God
Power and Glory
Pray for Israel
Prayer
Prosperity
Purity
Safe in My Father's Hand
Stay in your own Lane
Surrendered at your Feet
Taste and See
Thank you for my Healing
The Beginning of Easter
The Broad & Narrow Road
The Good News
The Mystery of Love
The One
The Power of God's Word
The Promise is Coming
The Truth
The Well
The Words of a Prayer
Three-fold Cord
Time
Traffic Lights
Treasures in Heaven
Waiting on God
Walking in the footsteps of my Love
Warrior Princess
Watchmen, it is Time!
What is the Church?
Why a Dark Church?
Why won't they Listen?
Will the Real Jesus please Stand Up!
You are my Peace
You are our Legacy
Your Hope
Your Love Never Ends

Introduction

I experienced a divine visitation during a youth camp when I was 14 years old in 1976. Jesus came to me and said, "I will never leave you; I will never forsake you." I had no idea that was a Bible verse, but His words struck a deep chord with me. It took me many years to discover that Jesus had maintained His promise to me throughout my life.

My second encounter with God occurred in 1988 when I was 26.. This took place in my bathroom. The accumulation of pain in my life had driven me to a dark place that I can only describe as hell on Earth. God appeared through the ceiling to show me His Sovereignty and amazing love.

The Holy Spirit flooded over my soul, giving me a brand-new existence. I was what the Bible refers to as "born-again." Those who have experienced salvation through Jesus Christ will understand what I am saying. For those who do not, I invite you to ask Jesus to make Himself real to you. God yearns for everyone to know Him and experience His love.

God told me in 1995 that I would write a book on my life journey. It would be my testimony to God's healing and redemptive plan for my life, which began with my conception in my mother's womb.

I never read books, so for me to write one would be a miracle. But when I braided the numerous colourful threads of my life, they created an astonishing design, one of which I needed to share.

And true to God's will for my life, in 2020, yes (that is 25 years of waiting on the Lord for His perfect timing), I published my book, My Child and the Tapestry of Life - A Destiny Woven for Victory. A Woman's Journey to Heal the Little Girl Inside.

Indeed, every colour was interwoven into the pattern of my life.

I'm grateful to everyone who connected with my story, expressed how reading it had an impact on their life, and mentioned how many of the experiences and hardships you went through were similar to mine. Knowing that my path has helped you in yours makes me feel grateful. Now, a sequel has been woven.

I'm thrilled to present a collection of poems. These other "Colourful Threads", in no particular chronological order, use poetry to express my life journey.

These poems are inspired by Bible passages, my own experiences, or things I've seen. Some have come from places of painful grief and unexpected betrayal. Others from waiting with years of stretched patience tarrying for promises.

Other threads were woven from overflowing joy, healing and bucketloads of love from God and others who are in my life and crossed my path. Other times God has revealed His heart to me, and I have captured His messages in rhyme.

I hope these poems, as they have done for me, will speak to your heart and inspire or challenge you as you read them. Savour the poetic expression of God's love for you and the design of Heaven's imprint on the pages that follow these very humble strands.

As I open my heart once more in complete transparency, may God bless you by adding hope, healing, redemption, and blessing to your life tapestry.

Thank you for holding "Colourful Threads" in your hands; may the words find their way into your heart and spirit deeply, lovingly, and profoundly.

I pray God showers you with His amazing love, and may you realise how faithful Jesus is, and that He will never leave you or forsake you.

Love Always,

Megan x

For we are the product of His hand,
heaven's poetry etched on lives,
created in the Anointed, Jesus to accomplish
the good works God arranged long ago.

- EPHESIANS 2:10 THE VOICE -

A Masterpiece

I am a simple strand of thread
In my Father's hand
And I must truly trust
Whatever He has planned
His colours for me are gold
His path for me is bright
He keeps me safe in the palm of His hand
I never leave His sight
Sometimes He weaves so tightly
I feel like I will break
And I am not exactly sure
How much pulling I can take
I see the underside at work
Frayed knots and tangled ends
Makes only sense my life's a mess
That never has an end
Then I turn the fabric over
To see my stitching story told
My Father's love planned all along
I am a Masterpiece foretold.

A New Door

God told me of a new door
That He has for me
It's ready to be opened
To bring great Victory!
To dreams, blueprints and visions
He's placed inside my heart
I have been praying for many years
For His promises to start
But God's been getting things ready
A foundation was being laid
He had to form my character
This couldn't be delayed
Betrayals, lies and gossip
These things did hurt me so
Satan had a field day
More than you'll ever know
But through the tears and heartache
God used these in my life
To bring a great endurance
Against these acts of strife
Before God takes you further
Into your next position
He always defeats those enemies
Bringing opposition
The joy of what is through the door
Is greater than I can say
Mourning turned to dancing
No more ashes in the way
I am just so expectant
This door in front of me
The next part to the journey
I just can't wait to see
And thank God for His timing

It's perfect, not like mine
He's never late or early
But always just on time
So, now I stand before this door
To open and reveal
All God's spoken promises
To come and be made real
Thank you, JESUS with all my heart
For giving me a story
And patiently outworking it
With mercy, grace and GLORY!

A New Year

As we begin a new calendar
I reflect on this past year
And the many trials I did endure
And the moments I held dear
There was good and there was bad
That's part of life I know
But the main thing I must remember
Is to be thankful as I sow
My gratitude and prayers to God
And how He's led me through
Always into Victory
His love for me is true
So, as I leave the old behind
And let go of last year
I set my gaze towards Heaven
In peace; I have no fear
God's given me dreams and visions
Blueprints deep inside
His word I keep before me
A lamp to where I stride
To pursue all God has for me
And fulfil His heart-planned call
To tell the world this message
His love's for one and all
So, come to Him just as you are
God has many things for you
Let your heart be filled with hope
And embrace this year anew.

A Perfect Life

I wanted my life to be perfect
From the inside out
Every tiny detail
Perfection was what it's about!
You see - when a child has trauma
Deep within their soul
To them - nothing but perfection
Will mend and make them whole
Every detail in it's place
This is what keeps them sane
But really - in 'reality'
It's impossible to obtain
It's almost like an OCD
Anxiety is your normal
You can't relax or just chill out
Everything has to be formal
I've been one who had such trauma
When I was just a child
It changed my whole demeanour
I became so meek and mild
So, on the outside you saw a smile
While deep within I cried
You only saw the happy mask
My life was one big lie
'A perfect life' I must control
It ate away at me
I desperately craved my freedom
Screaming inside to be free
Trauma is a horrible foe
And it changed me deep inside
The choices I couldn't help but choose
Trapped me for a very dark ride
I hate this life - why me -why me?
Why do I deserve all this?
I was so innocent way back then
My childhood should have been bliss

If there is a God up in the sky
Show me that you're real
I'll give you my heart, my soul, my life
If you come and help me heal
I need you deeply if you're there
Show yourself to me
And then… appearing so real and true –
JESUS! YES! YOU ARE HE!
You are the one I learned about
When I was very small
Before my life was darkened
Before satan took it all
Your Spirit is so beautiful
Healing me inside and out
Maybe no one will believe me
But from the rooftops, I want to shout!
Jesus, you are the Lord of lords
And King of all the kings
You took away my pain and shame
You're the reason my heart sings
There IS such a thing as a perfect life
Not one I make myself
But by simply being born-again
You'll restore my life to health
And every tiny detail
That I may care about
You bathe it with your pure true love
The darkness obeys your shout!
Your Power and Authority
And the Heavens they do roar
No one can tell me you're not real
I feel you to my core!
So, I let go of all my striving
For a perfect life for me
And I live in the perfection
Of God's love that sets me free.

Always There

I get up every morning
And dedicate my day
Into your hands Jesus
I need you in every way
You are the very air I breathe
You are my daily bread
You are the water to my soul
My spirit it is fed
Purely on your goodness
And your love for me
Whenever satan has me bound
You come and set me free
You promised that you'll stay with me
And never leave my side
I love you Holy Spirit
In you, I will abide
There is no mountain that's too high
No valley is too low
For when I need your help each day
With me, you'll always go
You are closer than a brother
And higher than a king
Better than a best friend
You are my everything
How blessed I am to know you
And you live inside my heart
You daily guide my every step
And repel the evil dart
That tries to bring me trouble
And cause my life much hurt
Your eyes are always on me
Your angels ready and alert

To come and help me when I need
The miracle for my prayer
You are Jesus, my Lord and Saviour
And you are always there!

Amazing Love

How can I put this into words?
To share your AMAZING LOVE
It's nearly indescribable
Your gift from Heaven above
Jesus, you are the Lord and King
But you came to die for me
You took my sin upon yourself
So, I could be made free
Then your Spirit searched high and low
You chased me down so hard
Relentless in your long pursuit
You showed me why you're scarred
It was because YOU LOVE ME
It's nothing I have done
It was God's plan all along
To crucify His son
Yes! It's all because YOU LOVE ME
Deep down to my core
And when the scales fell off my eyes
You showed me so much more
You showed me I'm forgiven
For all my deep dark sin
You washed me white with your red blood
Settling satan's score within
You set me free to love YOU
To be my long-lost Saviour
You cleansed and healed me in my soul
And changed my whole behaviour
Now every day when I awake
You are so very near
I put my TRUST in you alone
This world gives me no fear!
Because of your AMAZING LOVE

That runs deep in my soul
It's ONLY your AMAZING LOVE
That fills life's empty hole
Oh Lord you are my friend and King
That's how close you are to me
You whisper Heaven's secrets
While you rule with Royalty
Now I've found your AMAZING LOVE
I will never let you go
But tell the world that you exist
For them to also know
Of how you are pursuing them
As gentle as a dove
To touch their hearts and show them too
YOUR AMAZING LOVE!

An Ode for the Seer

I am a seer, don't get me wrong
I've accepted this gift in me
It's just some people think I'm crazy
To see the things I see
Some people sing and dance
Some are good at math
But I see clearly heaven's realm
And also satan's wrath
I write it down - I call it out
It's a risky thing to say
Some people they don't like it
It intimidates their day
For those who do not have this gift
They do not understand
That it's God who opens up my eyes
It's Him and not my plan
I've been rejected and misunderstood
Deemed crazy in my head
Keep away from 'that one'
She talks often with much dread
I've wrested daily with my life
What is wrong with me?
I don't think I am normal
I'm too sensitive you see!
I don't just see - I hear and taste
Feel, sense and even smell
All my senses are alight
And I have dreams as well
Other seers understand
And go through the same shame
And when we find each other
I'm encouraged once again
This is how God made me

And I really don't know why
I get many words and visions
To reveal His plans on High
I see demonic strategies
Assignments and evil schemes
I'm called to know and understand
What this darkness really means
God says that I'm a watchman
Waiting on the wall
To warn of approaching danger
So, others won't bear the fall
It's confusing and it's strange to some
As though I have two heads
Doctor's say I'm very strange
And offer me strong meds
So, I've leant that I am different
I'm a seer don't get me wrong
I now accept that's who I am
And in God's love I belong
So, that's okay I'm odd to you
But try to understand me
I see the spirit more than the norm
And friends I hope we can be
You do you and I'll do me
We are all a different being
I'll help you know the spiritual things
With my seers' gift of seeing.

Atmosphere Changer

Are you an atmosphere changer
When you walk into a room?
And sow seeds all around you
To grow and flourish and bloom
The essence that you carry
Will permeate the air
So, be sure you're planting good things
For others to be aware
That light expels all darkness
And faith replaces fears
Positive rids all negative
And joy removes all tears
What do you carry as your tune
When a melody is needed?
Hope and faith and all things sweet
What is it you've seeded?
I'll leave you this to ponder
When you next walk into a room
Does the atmosphere around you
Grow and flourish and bloom?

Basking in the Goodness of the Lord

I kneel before your Throne O Lord
I bow my head in prayer
I call to you; you answer me
For you are always there
Your presence descends upon me
And overwhelms my soul
Everything my life does lack
You touch and make me whole
You cleanse me on the inside
And wash away my sin
My anxious thoughts are finally at peace
Now your presence has settled within
I am consumed by your great love
As you overflow my heart
Lost in your great splendour
Lord, may we never be apart
For when I take this time to kneel
And show you; you're adored
Your love pours forth and I find myself
Basking in the goodness of the Lord.

Be Still
AND KNOW THAT I AM GOD

There is a place I want to be
And I will stay there till
I enter God's pure presence
Where I can be just still
And soak in my Father's love for me
Jesus died for this I know
He gave me the Holy Spirit
Everywhere I go
He is my true companion
The very best of friends
His love for me is always there
It never ever ends
So, when I want to soak in Him
I sit and wait until
He comes upon me like a dove
My heart and mind are still
And then I focus just on God
I breathe Him in so deep
Filling all my senses
His love I want to keep
With me always through the day
I seek Him for His will
And quieten to a place of rest
...and in Him, I am still.

Brand them Anew

If you could only see
The tricks of the enemy
He targets the mind
And he is not kind
And he's after you and me

But God has given us power
To fight him in this hour
His blood, his word
It must be heard
And the devil will run and cower

Stay strong in the Spirit
And courageous within it
You have everything you need
To stop his plans indeed
And walk with the Lord every minute

Victory is yours, Jesus paid it for you
Rise up and do what you're called to do
Go into the land
And take your stand
And deliver a people and
BRAND THEM ANEW.

Bullied No More!

Each time when I do see you
I shudder to my core
I can see you thinking
How can I hurt her more?
Evil lives inside your heart
And sin crouches at your door
I never know what's coming next
And what you have in store
I'm but a child and so naïve
You trick me every time
And woo me into your deep dark web
No way can I decline
So, this becomes my normal
And the way I see the world
That being hurt is just my life
With daily pain unfurled
Confusion blinds the way I think
I really am no good
Pain builds up within me
And I'm misunderstood
I cry out to be loved each day
And everywhere I go
I grow up looking for this love
With everyone I know
This serves me no real purpose
So, I try to ease the pain
With drugs and drink and harsh self-hate
To heal my heart again
There is no light my world is dark
I want to live no more
My self-hate grows inside me
And I'm darkened to my core
I'm desperate to escape this life

And cry to God on High
I hope my cries reach Heaven
Somewhere up into the sky
God answers me directly
He shows me His great love
This happens in the Spirit
This comes down from above
God sends His son called Jesus
To help me be set free
And by His very Spirit
God's love flows into me
And washes away my years of pain
The memories of my past
And all the bullies' tactics
Are washed away at last
This really is a miracle
That Jesus can do this
He came to die so I can live
The Bible's emphasis
It's been quite an unreal journey
Over many days and years
To heal from all my inner wounds
And release all of my fears
My inner child is finally healed
For the first time in my life
I have done lots of forgiveness
No more holding onto strife
But now my hope is renewed each day
God's love it falls on me
And Jesus helps me every step
Live my life in Victory!
No more – you bullies' – stay away!
Do not bother me!
I'm stronger than you'll ever know
I'm whole and happy and free!

Call Them In

Call them in from the east
And call them from the south
Stand upon the word of God
Declare it from your mouth
Call them from the west
And call them from the north
Come and stand upon God's word
Call them to come forth
And your prayers will dispatch angels
To disarm plans of the dark
Where satan and his demons
Want to leave their hate-filled mark
On those who are God's children
Though they have gone astray
Today we rise and we declare
COME BACK AND FIND YOUR WAY!
God is raising up a ROAR
A sound across this land
He's calling me – He's calling you
To come and make a stand
And speak with all authority
That Christ has given you
Declare the WORD with POWER
It is your sharp sword too
To cut away the strongholds
And the evil of this earth
Intercede with labour pains
Until VICTORY has been birthed
Come and join God's army
You're needed in this fight
The war against the darkness
Is won with Christ's great light

God wants His children to come home
Their broken hearts to mend
And through our prayers God's arms are wide
To love them once again.

Castles on the Sand

Lord, please hear my cry
Hear my desperate plea
Build my heart upon your Throne
And make me unto Thee
A home where you can live and reign
Deep within my heart
Start at my foundation
All my sins they must depart
I sweep them out my front door
And welcome in your Glory
I need your Spirit to change me
And give me a brand-new story
One to tell the world your truth
You came to die for all
Your love saves every person
From Adam and Eve's great fall
Build up my walls a safe place
Make them high and strong
Open wide my windows
So, all can hear my song
Build me a fortress on your Rock
So, when it's dark I stand
Make me a pure refuge
To help others in this land
That they will see the shining light
And Jesus, you're my source
You rescued me from evil days
And healed all my remorse
Now I choose very wisely
In how I build my life
Your word - my bricks and mortar
My prayers give me new life

My new home is your Kingdom
Who can understand?
I reach out to all who struggle
With their castles on the sand
Come build your life on Jesus
His Rock is very strong
And you will deeply know
This is where you belong
Don't worry about your mansion
While you're here on earth
There will be one in Heaven
Reserved with your new birth
You were born to build with God
A mighty destiny
God holds your unique blueprint
So, you can be set free
So come to Jesus
And lay it down
That He may lift your hand
And build you a strong tower
Not a castle on the sand
You will become a lighthouse
Filled with love and awe
And you will want to welcome
Others through your door
To find this one called Jesus
So, open up your heart
Receive His love and destiny
One step to your brand-new start.

Christmas Story

An angel came to shepherds
To announce a Saviour was born
It was a star that led three kings
To this baby to adorn
Bearing royal gifts of value
Frankincense, myrrh and gold
This wonderful Christmas story
Forever would be told
Of how little baby Jesus
Born God's son this day
Would fulfill every prophecy
His life would make a way
To bring healing and peace to everyone
Who calls upon His name
And if you give your life to Him
It will never be the same
What a gift God gave to us
For the whole world Jesus died
He gave His life so YOU can live
Forever by His side
Jesus is so very real
Just ask Him in your heart
The best gift ever given
Now God has done His part
So, as you enjoy this Christmas
With your family and your friends
Just remember Jesus
And how His story ends
He's coming back for those who love Him
Not a baby – but a King
And while you sing your carols
Know that THIS is why you sing

Have a very Merry Christmas
And enjoy this yuletide season
But never let this truth slip by
That Jesus is the reason.

Colourful Threads

God is the Master Weaver
Of all that's in the land
He spoke the Word in the beginning
Fashioned all from His Great Hand
Yes, that does include you and me
We were formed by His pure love
God knew you before the world began
Recorded in Heaven above
God wove you in your mother's womb
In that secret place
Your hands, your feet, your body
Your eyes, your hair, your face
Woven means embroidered
With many colourful threads
God knitted you so lovingly
You're perfect – He has said
You are woven with His beauty
And designed with dignity
You're predestined with a blueprint
An amazing destiny
So, never dislike what God has made
And who you are in life
Don't be negative about yourself
That only leads to strife
But treasure who you are, my friend
You're the apple of God's eye
He only fashions beautiful things
And that means you and I
So, when you're feeling sad and blue
And the world has so much dread
Focus on Creation
And look for the colourful thread

You'll see them all around you
God's woven tapestry
The hills, the grass, the sunsets
The sky, the land, the sea
Everything is just so perfect!
And designed with mastery
All is woven with God's beauty
Colourful threads for us to see.

Creation

What is this life all about?
Do you ever wonder why?
Who made the rivers on this land
The stars up in the sky?
There are so many roads to God
I hear those voices shout
It's my way or the highway
So now I'm full of doubt
I seek the truth, I want to know
How I came to be
Was it just the big bang?
Is that how life made me?
The Bible says I was created
By the hand of God
And really if I think on that
That's not at all quite odd
Also, it says in my mother's womb
In secret, I was woven
God was forming who I am
And in His heart, I'm chosen
That life is 'not' a mystery
It is made very clear
That Jesus is the path to take
His Spirit's always near
To those who have called upon His name
And given Him their heart
His love will lead and guide you
Then God will do His part
In showing you, He is the One
Who made rivers on this land
And put each star up in the sky
Now it's easy to understand

Because His love is - oh so real!
It's pure and it is free
And each day I live and breathe in Him
Because God has created me!

Daughter of the King

I'm not an orphan
In God's sight
He's purchased me
With a spiritual birthright
I am his servant
That is true
I seek to obey
In all I do
But there is a reason
My heart does sing
It is because
I'm a Daughter of the King
Abba Father
He calls me His own
I sit beside Him
On Heaven's Throne
His love encircles me
Day and night
I am so precious
In His sight
No more striving
And straining to please
I am His child
In peace; at ease
What a privilege
It is to be
God's special one
His love for me
His little girl
He looks to see
That I am blessed
Happy as can be
He pours down favour

And great blessing
I live my life
Without the stressing
God's placed on me
A Royal ring
I'm forever His
A Daughter of the King.

David and Goliath

David was but a shepherd boy
Tending to his sheep
Day and night he guarded them
He fought so he could keep
Them all safe and protected
Because he loved them so
The wilderness was his training
For little did he know
That God had bigger plans for him
One day he would be king
And guard over his people
Their praises to him sing
But he didn't know the future
He walked from day to day
Step by step in tune with God
Who guided him on his way
Now, there was this Goliath
An enemy in their land
And God had chosen David
With a slingshot in his hand
Goliath mocked God's people
And they were doomed for harm
But God had anointed David
And he was fearless and calm
Because he trusted in his God
Who'd given him victories before
The lion and the bear he'd slain
Now Goliath was one more
David arose and he declared
How dare you defy my Lord!
And with one mighty faith-filled swing
The rock he slung had bored

Right into Goliath's temple
And to the ground he fell
Defeating this whole army
Together with God so well
Because God is our true victor
When we have a foe
Something that defies our life
Stand up for all to know
That you are now brave David
Anointed and called on high
And when you wield your God-given sword
Your enemies will die
Because satan is your Goliath
And He defies our Lord
Satan wants you to fail and lose
In your God-given call
So, stand up mighty warrior
And use your authority
And bring down your Goliath
And walk fearless, strong and free.

Each Day is New

Every day is a NEW DAY
Created for us in a special way
Enjoy the blessings each day brings
Look for them hidden in many things
Delight, rejoice in the Lord always
And life will be wonderful as we gaze
God gives to us His gift of love
To make it through each day that's tough
Give His love that He gives to you
To others abundantly as EACH DAY IS NEW.

Encounter

It's not our job to judge the world
They can't help what they do
But we ARE called to watch and warn
And speak that which is true
Sin crouches in the darkness
And traps you unaware
To unassuming people
Who live without a care
And those who live for pleasure
Wrapped up in only self
Trapped in a spiritual blindness
Consumed by world's dark wealth
So, we who follow Jesus
The WAY the TRUTH the LIFE
Are here to warn of dangers
And lead you from sin's strife
You may not like what you will hear
As it challenges life's pleasures
But STOP and listen carefully
As we share God's greatest treasures
That God SO LOVED ALL in the world
He sent His only son
To die for ALL and set ALL free
Sin lost and Jesus won!
I pray you have an ENCOUNTER
That you meet Jesus, face to face
As He floods you with His love
You will see His Amazing Grace.

First Love

The day you touched my heart, Lord
It's so hard to describe
Your love for me so overwhelms
It's high, it's deep, it's wide
Your love for me is like no other
And my love is returned
Back to you, a consuming fire
Within my soul, you burn
Tears do flow out of me
Because your love's SO REAL
Your Spirit overshadows
Fills me with Heaven's zeal
I can't sit still, I need to speak
And tell the world your wonder
Your love is true, your love is pure
First love is what I'm under
Now I've known you thirty years
Since the day you touched my heart
We've travelled far, we've travelled long
Not once did you depart
Although our journey has been great
Some days have been a trudge
And I have lost my first love
The apathy would not budge
You say to stir it up again
This fire within my soul
And go back to my first love
The day you made me whole
I bow down low before you
And seek to see your eyes
Jesus, you are waiting
You are my only prize

Forgive me, Lord, for being so dim
Help me wherever I go
Because your love is like no other
No! Nothing else I know
So, I will put you first today
And open my heart in prayer
I will love you with my first love
Because your love is waiting there.

First Things First

Who wants to come second in life?
We're taught to always come first
We must get the ribbon with the number one
To quench our ego thirst
But God told me something important
As a key to our life in Him
That if we put GOD first in life
Then WE will surely win
Not just when we want to
Or when it suits us best
But obey His gentle leading
And God will do the rest
So let all else come second
If it stands before God's eyes
And then He will bestow on you
His crown that means FIRST PRIZE!

Forgiveness – I did choose

I had every reason
To hold my lifelong grudge
And no matter what had happened
Why should 'I' have to budge?
You see - there was 'this' time
And don't forget about 'that'
I couldn't let it go
So, I swept it under my mat
It hurt so much to think about
Such pain I had to bear
You tormented me day and night
And life was so unfair
My little mound of bitterness
Grew bigger when until
My little mound of yesterday
Had grown into a hill
It could go on no longer
I had to finally see
To forgive, I'll loose the grip of pain
And in time - be a memory
But my thoughts raged inside my head
Black bitterness filled my soul
The poison kept on pouring in
I am trapped in this dark hole
And now my hill inside me
Was mountain size instead
It brought me pain and sickness
Anguish never left my head
I had to climb my mountain
It was so high and wide
It seemed to take a long, long time
Now, determined in my stride
When I reached the top and looked down

At 'this' time and at 'that'
It was so far away
I could hardly see the mat!
Resentment - you are not my friend
I have to let you go
Your poison I refuse to drink -
Today I will say NO!
I released all of my hatred
I let it fall away
"Don't come back, let me be free"
For now, and every day
Sometimes thoughts still remind me
Though their sting now doesn't last
The gesture of forgiving you
Is 'my gift' for 'your past'
Looking back, I'm finally free
It's my gain, and you lose
Your power and pain over me – no more
Forgiveness - I did choose.

Getting it Right

All my life I've got it wrong
By making TRAUMA CHOICES
It was because of years of hurt
And hearing negative voices
BUT after layers of God's healing
DEEP within my life
God melted away all of my pain
And removed memories of strife
NOW I'm ready to GET IT RIGHT
My life is not my own
Because I've TOTALLY surrendered
And with Jesus, I'm NEVER alone
So, now HE guides me THE RIGHT WAY
I FOLLOW where He leads
Making my crooked paths straight again
His GENTLE voice I heed
I LOVE my Jesus who is so gentle
My Shepherd who guides me now
Into a future I can't describe
Most days I just say…WOW!
More than I can imagine or dream
Good things God has for me
NO MORE trauma choices
Just JOY-FILLED VICTORY!

God is Listening
DEDICATED TO KOMAL AND GOHAR ALMAS

God is listening
He is ALWAYS there
He hears your whispers
Your heartfelt prayers
God is listening
He sees it ALL
And when you cry out
He won't let you fall
But the world is a mess
He hears you say
I cannot live another day
Put your trust in God
The One above
And He will cover you
With His love
It may seem dark
And there is no end
God has a plan
And He will contend
And bring the VICTORY
Over you
There is absolutely nothing
God cannot do
To keep you safe
From these evil days
Just bend your knee
Let him hear you say
Of ALL your worries
Your dreams and fears
Tell Him the now
And yesterday years
For God is listening

And He has a plan
To deliver you out
From the hands of man
A SOVEREIGN God
He wants you to know Him
A powerful God
His light shall not dim
So, trust in Jesus God's one TRUE son
Hope in the cross
For ALL He has done
And you shall be free
Set apart in His light
The dark cannot touch you
You are His delight
God is listening
He is always there
He will answer your whispers
Your heartfelt prayers.

Created into a song in 2022 by Gohar Almas
Listen on YouTube: *God is Listening – Gohar Almas*

God is Love

Did you know that God is love?
And He wants to live IN you!
He created the heavens and the earth
There is nothing He can't do
Except invade upon our will
God has given us free choice
He wants us ALL to cry aloud
And reach Him with our voice
And ask Him to reveal to us
The reason we are here
And God will whisper deep within
Because YOU are so dear
He will tell us of His undying love
That He's given us His son
God will speak this truth to us
So, our hearts will be undone
Jesus was God's long-term plan
Created from the beginning
He is the BRIDGE that fills the void
To take away our sinning
He makes us pure and holy
And stand strongly in His GRACE
It's now because of Jesus
That we can see God's face
Shining down upon us
Dwelling in our heart
Now we reside together
And we will never part.

God-blessed Ride!

Never give up believing
On your dreams tucked down inside
Even when they seem too big
Too high, too deep, too wide
For you to ever reach them
Impossible it seems!
But I'm here to say – never give up!
On your visions, goals and dreams
Because even though they take a while
Or you don't believe they'll come
Don't give up on praying for them
And never say, "I'm done!"
For God has given you these dreams
They are His very best
It's in the wait that you endure
And pass His faith-filled test
Everything will be so wonderful
He's working behind the scenes
Just wait for God's perfect timing
It's closer than it seems
So, hope and trust and don't let go
Keep telling God your point
And in time and due season
Your dreams will not disappoint
The last thing here that I will say
Is TRUST and just stand by
God will bring your heart's desires
It's in hindsight, you'll know why
Although it might be tempting
To lose all hope inside
Just keep your prayers and faith aflame
And get ready for a God-Blessed Ride!

God-given Gift

What is your God-given gift?
The Lord has given you
Can you sing? Can you dance?
What stirs your life so true?
What makes you, YOU! I'm asking?
In a special way?
What unique talents
Thrill your heart today?
What do you dream about at night?
When the business is still
What passion lies inside you?
What drives your inner will?
Because whatever it is you love to do
Deep within your soul
I can guarantee one thing
To do that will make you whole
No longer to be empty
Or bored with everyday
Coz when you do the thing you love
Great passion will light the way
Your gift and call inside you
Will grow for all to see
And God has this one purpose
For you to live in Victory!
So, don't hide it under a bushel
Or bury it in the sand
Don't be lazy and with-hold
What God's placed in your hand
But flourish and grow and bloom within
It is your God-given call
And when you use it daily
Blessings will flow to all.

God's Glory Train

Come and ride God's GLORY Train
And you will never be the same
For as you board, you will see
Creation's wonders for you and me
Buy your ticket, there is a price
The cost is love, that will suffice
Your love for God, His love for you
The two entwined in Heaven's dew
The Spirit comes down to create the story
And breathes a wind that brings in the Glory
The Glory is HOLY, it's pure, it's sweet
Falling down on your knees, bowing low at God's feet
The GLORY is gentle, so soft and healing
Tears will flow, it's a beautiful feeling
The Glory has power, it's weighty and strong
You stand before God, it's where you belong
So, line up my children, press into God's heart
Don't be a fool, but rather be smart
Don't lose your ticket, your invite to board
Come and make Jesus your Saviour and Lord
Come and ride God's GLORY Train
And you will never be the same
For as you board, you will see
Creation's wonders for you and me.

God's Holy Fear

What is the fear of the Lord?
Some say it's wisdom, some understanding
But don't be flippant
With scriptures demanding
To bow down low before your King
And give your heart
To praise and sing
Of all the wondrous deeds of God
Even if others say you're odd
They live their lives, each to their own
They revel in their flesh
And then they moan
Of never ever having enough
They see their lives
As hard and tough
But those who seek after God's own heart
And deny their flesh
Their lives set apart
For God's eyes only
His Spirit and word
They are the ones
Who live free as a bird
Because they fear with all their might
And desire to bow
And live holy and right
In fear and surrender
To Jesus their Lord
And in return
They're favoured and adored
With peace in their heart
And grateful for the small
Their joy is full

To answer God's call
One thing that differs between the two
Some disregard what Jesus can do
When you bow down low
Holy Spirit comes near
And you live a blessed life
In GOD'S HOLY FEAR.

God's Love for Me

I get up every morning
And sit before your throne
I bare my soul towards you
My life is not my own
Your Spirit pours down upon me
Flowing from Heaven above
Your still and gentle presence
Saturate me with your love
Tears flow freely down my face
And I humbly do receive
All your mercy and your grace
It's impossible to conceive
The magnitude of your power
Your hope, your life, your peace
The ever-present love of Jesus
For me that will never cease
Why me and what did I do
For your love to save my life?
But I'm so grateful every day
That you took away my strife
No more am I plagued with hopelessness
And all-consuming fear
Because your never-ending love
Is always very near
No matter what valley or mountain I climb
You are with me every step
You said you'd never leave me
And you haven't done so yet
No more in the kingdom of darkness
For your death upon the cross
Took away my every sin
Satan's grip on me was lost
Because your blood you shed for me

Is so powerful and great
Satan's works of evil
Will not direct my fate
You set me in your Holy place
In the Kingdom of Your Light
Where I behold your Glory
Every day and every night
So, every morning as the sun shines in
You're the beginning of my day
I sit in peace, in your sweet love
And forever it's where I'll stay.
AMEN!

P.S.
Good morning blessings
To you Lord
I can't help but tell you
How much you're adored!
I ADORE YOU!

God's Love is Coming

God knows what He is doing?
Child of God – do not fret
Do not fear and do not doubt
Don't look backwards with regret
But stand firm on the word of God
It's trusted and it's true
He's the God of the impossible
There's nothing He can't do
Whether stuck down in the valley
Or trapped in a stronghold
God is working on your behalf
To bless you sevenfold
Cry out to Him in anguish
Be true to how you feel
Don't wear a mask and then pretend
Your trial is no big deal
God wants you to be honest
For you to bare your soul
Be truthful and authentic
It's the way you will be whole
God is at the ready
To take all of your prayers
And though He might feel far away
He's close and He does care
God has a perfect plan in mind
To turn your trial for good
Don't doubt His Sovereign Genius
His plan misunderstood
But TRUST your Father will come through
In POWER and in GRACE
And level every valley
Every stronghold He'll displace
And turn around your circumstance

As only God can do
In His way and His timing
His word is sure and true
So, look up child of God this day
Raise your eyes above the doom
And know GOD'S LOVE IS COMING
To deliver you very soon.

God's Planned Call

All my life satan has been
Trying to thwart my call
Doing everything he can
To try and make me fall
He struck me right inside the womb
Trying to destroy my life
My mother self-aborted me
But I survived that knife
Then I was tormented
By a family member
Years and years I suffered harm
Too many to remember
Damaged, broken and full of fear
I ventured into life
My daily trauma choices
Brought nothing more than strife
I encountered many men
Who did me very wrong
Many times, I tried to end my life
For nowhere did I belong
Then one day I met another man
It was JESUS to be sure
He healed and loved me purely
Right deep inside my core
He gave my life a purpose
And said I had a call
That He would never leave me
Or ever let me fall
Satan's tried as I have said
To stop the very thing
That God wants me to do for Him
My service to the King
But my God is so faithful

And Jesus is so true
Satan's plans will not succeed
Whatever he tries to do
The Bible is my instruction
God's word my very sword
I will yield it as a prayer
With Jesus Christ my Lord
Satan will be defeated
Though his battles they come fast
God is my defender
The devil will always come last
As God is Sovereign over you
He covers you with His hands
Victory will be daily yours
To live in your call God's planned
So, nobody or nothing
Can stop or even sway
God's Almighty Power
From fulfilling YOUR CALL God's way.

Heart Shine Check

Am I walking with Christ Jesus?
Or am I doing just what I please?
WWJD is real
Is the Bible a really big deal?
I am a Christian
I'll pull up my socks
I'll stop playing games
Not be one who mocks
What Jesus did for me on the cross
Because living so frivolously
It's my great loss
I need to be full of His Spirit and glowing
And walk in God's love – full to overflowing
With mercy and goodness
And blessings untold
When I am young
And when I am old
I must heed the call of God's perfect love
And live in the Spirit from Heaven above
Step into this realm
I will do it by choice
And stop listening to satan
And following his voice!
I'll AWAKE and ARISE
And stop being so lazy
I'll open my Bible
To truths that amaze me
What will it take for me to lay down
My worldly desires
And straighten my crown?
The love of the Father
Is waiting at my door
So, I'll open it wide

For God to give me more –
More of His love
His goodness, His grace
I'll witness His Glory
And see His great face
Shining towards me
My life it will be
Turned around every day
In full victory!
I'll surrender to Jesus
Now is the time
And the Spirit will fill me
And make my heart shine!

Heart Weavers

DEDICATED TO ALL THE BEAUTIFUL HEARTWEAVERS

God has sent beautiful women
To stand with me in life
They have my back and pray for me
To combat satan's strife
We are a team called Heart Weavers
God gathered us through His heart
And gave to us a blueprint
For us to do our part
To help all those with trauma
And living in despair
God has come to rescue those
Trapped in a deep dark lair
We will gather around you
And teach you many things
From practical to spiritual
You're a Daughter of the King
Beautiful are these Heart Weavers
And pure in heart they are
Loving God with their whole being
Ready to advance so far
In our Kingdom purpose
Of Love and Share and Care
Building a loving community
Through the Power of much prayer
I am so very grateful
God wove us all together
And now I call us family
In His Kingdom plan forever!

Hero Unaware

Are you called to be a HERO
By Almighty God?
You might think you are nothing
Or as some say, "a little odd"
But I have something to whisper
To those who have an ear
Something quite incredible
So, stop and come, draw near
Of what I have to share with you
From God's throne and His WORD
It will be quite spectacular
You may not have seen or heard
The Great plans and adventures
Your Destiny God's carved out
For you to fulfil upon this earth
Just believe and do not doubt
He's called you to be mighty
Stand strong upon this earth
Dreams and visions and blueprints
Inside you, God has birthed
You may feel insignificant
Treated badly, and that's unfair
But deep down there inside you
Lies a HERO UNAWARE
So, rise up in the POWER of God
He's called you to be strong
Walk daily on the path in front
Even though the journeys' long
And in time and due season
God's plan will soon unfold
Your hidden life now can shine
And be forever told
Who you are and what you do

For God is oh-so-great
Your life, your struggles and your joys
So many will relate
And you will make a difference
It's what God's called you to
No more HERO UNAWARE
The hour has risen on you
Now, go and make your legacy
Go and pave the way
So, you will encourage others
When it is their day
Rise up, HERO UNAWARE
And stand strong in your gift
The future is yours to change for God
Many things that you will shift
And put in place God's destiny
Yes, He has used your hand
To be a channel for His love
Now the HERO – YOU UNDERSTAND!

His Love

How He loves me so
My precious Lord and Saviour
Jesus came to me one night
And gave me so much favour
Someone must have prayed for me
In my family line
It is because of their faithful prayers
That I was saved in time
Jesus, He came after me
And showed me God is real
Not just with much head knowledge
But in my heart, I feel
This Amazing Love I talk about
I hope you feel it too
Now I'm the one who's praying
That salvation comes to you!
And Jesus will follow you around
Everywhere you go
Drawing you daily with His truth
His love for you to know
I won't give up on praying
I love you, don't you see
And when you come to Jesus
We will share eternity
Together, forever our spirits will live
That's God's promise in His word
Everlasting life is ours
This truth needs to be heard
All it takes is a step of faith
Towards God's Heavenly Throne
And give your heart and life to Him
Then you'll never be alone

Because Jesus will be your very best friend
He'll show you that He is real
And bless you with much favour
His Amazing Love you'll feel.

Honour

Have you ever been dishonoured?
Somewhere in your life
I bet it did feel awful
And only led to strife
Well, let me share right here and now
That's not the heart of God
He doesn't rule with an iron fist
And beat you with a rod
No! God, He wants to love you
And sees your gifts within
He wants you to succeed in life
Despite all your past sin
And share His loving heart with you
Great love, it will abound
And all will come to know God's love
And hear true honour's sound
Honour says "You're valuable"
"And your life has great meaning"
"You are gifted with many talents"
Jesus Christ is our redeeming
He sets our feet upon His rock
And though we're jars of clay
We're filled inside with precious gold
To shine God's love display
And all God's wonderful goodness
And His plan for me
Nothing can dishonour
For I am finally free
Of all my past and sin and shame
They are forgiven at the cross
Don't let anyone ever treat you
With disrespect and loss

For Great is our Redeemer
And He honours who we are
So, stand up tall and live for Christ
And He will honour us far.

Hope

How can people just not see
The state the world is in?
Satan's running rampant
Enticing us to sin
And go against God's purity
That started in the garden
Satan told Eve it was all okay
That God would surely pardon
But disobedience to God's word
Is never all okay
And repeated sin through history
This is where we are today
God says it's not okay to kill
But we do so in the womb
We take away a human's life
For them, it's way too soon
God says it's not okay to lust
And sleep with your same sex
He's made us man and woman
To procreate His best
God says it's not okay to lie
To rob, kill and destroy
These are fruits of satan
His tactics to deploy
And some who hold great power
With position and much wealth
Control the way we live our lives
Which in turn affects our health
They tell us how to live and think
Through subtle propaganda
And we become extremely numb
To discern their wicked slander
If we don't wake up and call them out

They'll have total authority
Over our minds and DNA
We will never be free
So, cry out to the greater one
In Power and Majesty
God Almighty in the Heavens
HIS final authority
To expose this wicked agenda
And reveal all satan's plans
That started in the garden
To destroy the life of man
For God so loved the world
He gave His only son
And if we call on Jesus
Our battles will be won
So even though this world's a mess
There is HOPE in front of you
Grab hold of all God's promises
And see what He will do
One day this evil it will stop
A new earth God will send
And all our pain and suffering
Will be brought to a final end
Choose the way of righteousness
Jesus is the ONLY way
To rid this world of evil
And let it start today!

I am a City on a Hill

You are calling me to shine my light
For all the world to see
You are calling me for my faith to be bright
What my Saviour did for me
Jesus grabbed me out of my darkness
And into His Kingdom of Light
Jesus filled me with His love
And turned my wrongs to right
Satan thought that He had won
On the cross when Jesus died
But then He rose into the sky
Forever by God's side
To pour down from Heaven's Throne room
A faith and peace so still
His way, His truth, His love
Now forever I am filled
You are calling me to shine my light
For all the world to see
And be A CITY ON A HILL
Shining forth my Victories.

I am Free!

Jesus, you are the one I search for
Deep in my soul when my days are dark
Jesus, you are the one I long for
To erase away every single black mark -
That was etched upon me
Without my consent
Inflicted by one
Whose rules were bent
SET ME FREE, SET ME FREE
Is my cry deep inside
Expose the root
No longer will you hide
And the light of God
Will shine so bright
And the truth of the matter
Will be made right
God's love will heal me
And set me apart
To heal my soul,
My body, my heart
No more will I fear
The terror of the night
All those demons have now
Gone to flight
God's love for me
Is deeper than my pain
Never, ever will I
Be trapped again
The gift of FREEDOM
Has come to my need
WHO THE SON SETS FREE
IS FREE INDEED!

I will Always Remember

I will always remember God
The day you became real in my life
Your love came and touched my heart
A heart so full of strife
You showed me Jesus – your beautiful son
You opened my eyes to what He had done
Being with His disciples, bread and wine in a cup
He said His goodbyes – His life to give up
His body was beaten – His blood was poured out
His Spirit left Earth with a final shout
God – you loved me so much that you allowed Jesus to die
To wash away my sin that blocked you and I
Jesus' death was so cruel, so painful, so unfair
But you wanted me, Father
That's how much you care
For today and forever I have Jesus your son
Living inside me – God that's what you've done
I will always remember God each time I mess up
Or go back to my old sin and take a sip from 'that' cup
When I feel so bad that I've let you down
I see Jesus on the cross with his painful crown
Then your arms wrap around me and squeeze me so hard
I know you love me – I know why Jesus was marred
I will always remember when my life fell apart
My body was sick, broken was my heart
My children were fatherless and I was alone
The bills were so high and I couldn't pay the phone
God, you surrounded me and met me again
Waves of your love flowed over my pain
And I knew in my head and with thanks in my soul
Why Jesus had died – so I could be whole
I will always remember you, Father, day after day

I will love you forever and I'll do what you say
I now drink from a new cup the one Jesus said
And to thank Him I take this wine and this bread
Thank you, my Father for sending your son
I will always remember what Jesus has done.

I will get There

Oh Lord, one more day
The journey is so long
One more day
Another line to add to my song
One more day
A memory for tomorrow
One more day
Of ending my ageing sorrow
Some days they are not easy
And others – they just slip by
But I have my gaze on Jesus
His words are in my eye
I rejoice and hope and live in Him
Fulfilling the hours around
Getting to know God's wonderful Grace
And the Holy Spirit's sound
How much there is I have to learn
How small I really am
I have so very far to go
To become just who I am
I can only breathe because of love
That God shines down on me
I will survive this path of mine
It's CHRIST who makes me free.

1. Jesus will Return!

The Bible speaks of my return
At the end of Revelation
To a world that is slowly dying
To every tribe and nation
Earthquakes, fires and many wars
Are birth pains can't you see?
The beginning of many sorrows
Before my return of Victory!
Many of you who do believe
Are waiting for my return
But sadly, there are also many
Who just have never learned
About my love and how I died
To save them from their sin
Satan runs this world you know
And has planted lies within
Every school around the world
He's taught against Creation
That it was evolution
Not God through His elation
And love and power and joy for man
To create all in His likeness
So, therefore many have been robbed
From knowing the Father's kindness
Some think Christmas is for Santa
And lollies and elves and deer
Many never know the truth
On Christmas Day I'm near
And many don't know about Easter
How I died upon the cross
And rose again in strength and power
To save all who are lost

So, that is why I'm coming back
For my remnant who love me
What a Great and Terrible Day to come
For every eye will see
The truth we tried to tell them
About my life and death
And how my Father loves them
All those upon the earth
So – are you ready for my return?
Ask me in your heart
And when the hour that I do come
A new life with me you'll start
Don't live in confusion anymore
But look for my return
You'll know this is the truth I speak
By your heart which longs and yearns
Day and night my consuming love
It keeps you safe and sound
And one day my child we will stand together
Once lost but now you're found
Be open to this truth I share
Listen, glean and learn
Because one day the world will surely see
The magnificence of my return!

If you only knew...

If you only knew
How much God loves you
You would fall to your knees
If you only knew
How much Jesus cares for you
You would let go of all your fears
If you only knew
God can heal your broken heart
You would place it in the palm of His hand
If you only knew
God is your loving Father
You would sit in total peace in His presence
If you only knew
Jesus died so you can have eternal life
You would run into His loving arms
If you only knew
That salvation and a new life are real
You would receive His gift with thankfulness
If you only knew...

It's not too Late

It's not too late to come to God
Any day of your life
Even if you think you've lived
An existence full of strife
No one's too bad or ever too lost
To receive God's love it's true
Did you know it's because of Jesus
He died in the place of you?
Jesus washed away your sin
When He hung upon the cross
It was God's plan all along
So, you would not be lost
Oh, see the Father's love for you
It's powerful and it's free
His love is never-ending
He loves unconditionally
God will never turn His back
His arms are open wide
Turn and come towards Him
Stop trying to run and hide
For nothing will ever satisfy
Your soul with any peace
Until you surrender to God's love
Your darkness will never cease
So, never think it is ever too late
To come to God again
Even if you've walked away
It doesn't matter when
But make the choice right here and now
Deep within your heart
Step into God's Kingdom
You'll be blessed with a brand-new start!

Jesus is Calling

I hear Jesus say my name
He has for me a call
I will surrender completely to Him
And give to Him my all
I will leave behind me
The things that hold me back
All of life's distractions
That cause my heart to lack
Love and fervour for my King
God does require from me
All my TRUST and OBEDIENCE
These things bring victory
God has for me a grand plan
A blueprint you might say
There is a whole wide world out there
Crying to be saved
Equipped with gifts and favour
I'll do my very best
To hear the whispers of my Lord
And He will do the rest
To lead me in my mission
To share God's love to all
And help them also understand
They too have a call
So, tune your ear to the sound
Of Jesus calling you
Because you need to understand
There's a work for us to do
To share the heart of God to those
Who desperately need His love
So, one day they will also hear
Their name called from heaven above.

Jesus is the Reason

You've heard it said
Once or twice
At Christmas time
Are you naughty or nice?
Well, this is true
If it's Santa Claus
But just stop a minute
And listen and pause
To ponder the truth
Of the Christmas season
It is because
JESUS IS THE REASON!
Yes, He came as a baby
And was born in a manger
Receive Him as King
No more a stranger
He decorated a tree
With his life He gave
Jesus shed His blood
So, we could be saved
So, as we celebrate
His birth this year
Take a moment and reflect
In between your cheer
That while it's fun
With elves and Santa
Don't get distracted
With all the banter
Focus on the true
Meaning of this season
And always hold dear that
JESUS IS THE REASON!

Just Believe

JUST BELIEVE!
That's all you need
To move the mountain
Into the sea
JUST BELIEVE!
That's all you need
I AM who I say I AM
JUST BELIEVE!
That's all you need
To SEE ME
To KNOW ME
To LOVE ME
JUST BELIEVE!
That's all you need
Things can change in 'one moment' in time
JUST BELIEVE!
That's all you need
To change the direction of your life
JUST BELIEVE!
That's all you need
I hold the whole world in my hands
And YES –
That includes YOU
JUST BELIEVE!
That's all you need
To be safe in my plans
That are good and sure
JUST BELIEVE!
That's all you need
To be by my side
For ALL eternity
JUST BELIEVE!

Just say Yes!

One day the Lord, He called me
To serve Him all my days
He gave to me a blueprint
To walk in all His ways
Some say that I am chosen
But wait – you just might guess
God doesn't have a favourite
All I said – was – YES!
So, if you want to serve God
But don't know where to start
Just say YES to God right now
And He will set you apart!
Then you will do the Great things
For His Kingdom plans, not less
All because you made the choice
And gave the Lord, YOUR YES!

Keep Me Anchored

In the beginning, You made the earth
And the Heavens are the work of your hand
You called my name, to be your child
Now in your truth, I stand
Show me your ways, your light, your love
I need to follow your word
I need to fill myself every day
And know my prayers are heard
Life – it gets very hard at times
Challenges are all around
But keep me anchored in your love
And your mercy to me abound
The meaning of your anchor
Is hope deep in my soul
It will keep me firmly tied to you
Your truth will make me whole
You will never let me go
Jesus, always by my side
It's your promise and your truth
In your hope, I will abide
Nothing can ever take me
Out of your loving hand
Because you will keep me anchored
And together we will stand
Forever as my ABBA God
Always in my heart
No storms or winds of hopelessness
Can tear our love apart
So, keep me anchored in your love
It's where I long to be
And we will be tied together
For all eternity.

Kingdom RAC

Are you a member of the RAC?
No! Not the motoring kind
Let me explain just what I mean
And see what you will find
That in my explanation
Using these few letters
They will spell out something else
That is so much better.
R is for Radical!
In the Kingdom realm
You're sold out for your Saviour
His love does overwhelm
A is for Available!
Any time of day
You hear God's voice so clearly
And follow in His way
C is for Christian!
It means Christ lives in you
You died to your old self
And travel life's road anew
So, let's put it all together
RADICAL AVAILABLE CHRISTIAN
Are you a member of this club?
And live from this position
Because if you're not I say to you
Join up it's just so easy
Believe that Jesus died for you
For God, this did appease He
Because God Almighty loves you
So, be a lifelong member
Of the Christian Kingdom
Forever to be remembered
And live with this assurance

Every time that you break down
Or feeling flat and empty
And life is one big frown
That you can call God's number
No call-out fee applied
No wait or any distance
He'll be swiftly by your side
To fix your life and repair your loss
And get you on the road
With God, you will then journey
No more a heavy load
I wouldn't be without this
My Kingdom RAC
For life I have this promise
God will be there when I need
I'm a Radical Available Christian
Travelling with my Lord
And life is one big adventure
When Jesus is on board!

Letting Go

One day I looked inside of me
To see who was actually there
Among the many things I saw
Was a little girl full of despair!
Why are you so sad? I asked
Shouldn't your pain be gone?
Didn't Christ die for you
So, there would be nothing wrong?
I can't get out she won't let go
I've been trapped in here for years
I don't know why she hangs onto me
I bring her nothing but tears
It's a war sometimes inside of her
I don't know what to do
I'm tired of fighting the same old war
That I really should not have to
If only she knew that Jesus is here
Saying all the time
Let go of it and all past pain
So that you truly can be mine
He tells her all the time you know
And most times she doesn't hear
But hides behind me like a friend
When I'm the one she should fear
One day I hope she stops very still
To look and see the lie
That I'm no friend just years of pain
And I hope she'll let 'ME' die
And let JESUS inside of her
Take my place instead
To be her friend and comforter
In her heart not just her head
He will never hurt her
Or do her any wrong

He will fill her big black gap
With love that truly belongs
To be her needed portion
To fill her space of pain
One day I'd like to see her
Be that happy person again
If she only knew how different
JESUS can make her be
By replacing HIS trust and love
Instead of hanging onto me
Inside her He'd plant a garden
With seeds of strength and peace
And water it with hope and love
His nurture would never cease
And in time and due season
Would soon grow and appear
Little buds of happiness
That would blossom from year to year
They would look so very pretty
With scent so wonderfully sweet
And bring much joy and healing
Making her complete
If only she would trust
And give JESUS ALL HER PAIN
She would never have
A hurting heart again
Maybe you can tell her
Since you know her very well
The next time that you look inside
Find a moment just to tell
To let go of the old
And plant within her soul
New faith seeds of happiness
That will grow and make her whole.

Lord, I'm getting older!

Where has my body gone?
Now I'm getting old
My mother never said anything
Why wasn't I told?
That at the age of 50
I would heat and sweat
And all my clothes would hang on me
Because I've made them wet
Then there is the weight gain
Don't even get me started
It's like the old me has completely gone
Where have I departed?
It is all just so confusing
My moods they come and go
Who is this new person?
I'd really like to know
And then at night when I'm trying to sleep
I toss and turn and sweat
And then I've done it all again
This time the sheets are wet
I get really bloated
From only breathing air
I've now become a size 16
How is this even fair?
But then I talk to all my friends
And yes, we have a giggle
I'm not the only one whose tummy
Does a little jiggle
So, here's to getting older
I have accepted it now
That grey hairs do bring wisdom
And that's comforting somehow

So don't mind me as I get old
Don't panic and do not rush
I'm not dying or even having a fit
It's just a very HOT FLUSH!

Lord, I'm Listening

God speaks every day to us
In nature all around
He tells us of His Sovereignty
As everywhere He's found
He's the very air we breathe each day
He's the mountains and the sky
God is in all creation
It's easy to see why
That it's because He loves us
He created us from the earth
And now it is God's lifelong quest
For us to have new birth
By His very Spirit
He longs for us to be
A precious, unique child of God
And be part of His family
Through Jesus Christ, His begotten son
Who gave His life for you
This is how God speaks to us
To declare His love so true
So, if you want to hear God's voice
The Bible makes it clear
Read the scriptures and pray to God
He will speak and you will hear
And tell you that He loves you
Each and every day
Just go outside and look around
Breathe deep His love today
Lord, I'm ready and I'm listening
With my ears to hear your sound
And know your love surrounds me
In Creation to be found.

Lord, I Pray

Jesus taught us how to pray
To His Father who reigns on High
And how to bring our hearts to Him
In God, we can rely
We first and foremost honour Him
And elevate God's name
Then recognise His Kingdom come
On earth to be the same
Then we bow to God's perfect will
It's the centre of our being
And thank Him for our daily bread
We believe without ever seeing
To forgive our sins and trespasses
For us and our enemies
And we are told to do the same
If we want to see Victories!
And lead us not into temptation
But deliver us from evil
And we will see God's mighty hand
Giving us peace to be still
For Thine is the Kingdom
The Power and the Glory
Forever and Ever!
AMEN.

Lost Anointing

Where did your anointing go?
I would really like to know
Why have you lost God's precious Grace?
And why has God now turned His face
Away from all you do and say
Why have you seemingly lost your way?
I know why you have no favour!
It's because of your fleshly behaviour!
My heart it grieves as now I look
To see you not living by the good book
You have let go of God's great plan
And bowed your knee to the works of man!
You have no power, no Holy Oil
You scheme and plan in human toil
The 'works of man' would now surmise
The way you live – yourself is your prize
All I can do is pray for you
For God to show you what to do
No longer bringing His LIGHT and GLORY
For now, you are writing your own story
Please repent, surrender, be humble
Before God makes your whole life crumble
It's not too late, please turn today
Your heart and life towards God's way...

Love and Unity

Oh, my children – please get along
And forgive each other for what was done wrong
No one is perfect in this world
Especially when sin is unfurled
Yes, they hurt you and you hurt them
But you must let go and forgive once again
Justice and vengeance are mine to deal
Trust in my WORD and not what you feel
Of course, it's okay to put boundaries in place
In fact, it's a must, but do it with grace
Forgive and let go of your troubles inside
Bless them abundantly – let go of your pride
At the end of the day, you must count the cost
Don't get distracted or you will be lost
My burden is easy and my yoke is light
Just say you're sorry to make it all right
In the realm of eternity, it's really quite small
So, lift up your eyes and let go of it all
And you will find freedom and hope for your soul
And live in a world with peace to behold.

Love, Share and Care

There is something that I live by
Everyhow and everywhere
To everything I say and do
I must love, share and care!
They did this in the Bible
Many years ago
Jesus taught His followers
So, they will surely know
That God's two new commandments
Were all to do with love
First and foremost, it is God
Our Father up above
Then, well it's your neighbour
That's every human heart
God wants us to love people
We need to do our part
In sharing and caring for others
It's how God spreads His love
God will teach us through His Spirit
Just follow the white dove
By doing this we're pleasing God
Life's not just all about self
To love and care for others
Will bring to earth great wealth
One thing I will remember
When I've said 'YES' to my call
Is to love and share and care for those
Spreading God's pure love to all.

Ministry behind the Mask

God called me into Ministry
Before I knew the task
But nothing could prepare me
For Ministry behind the mask
I can see you smile at me
And your tongue drips pleasant words
But right behind that smile, there is
An agenda that is quite blurred
I didn't see it coming
When you told so many lies
About me to other people
I know – as God has spies
To show me truth along the way
It's not always as it seems
I should have listened to my gut
And not your fancy gleams
How does this even happen?
When those in authority bend
To satan's plans and agendas
And to his schemes they send
Great untruths about me
What have I done to you?
I just answered God's call for me
What else should a Christian do?
Why such opposition?
From even my own kind
You're meant to be my family
Not stab me from behind
But God says I'm to bless you
And send forgiveness your way
And pray you see what you have done
It's sinful unfair play

But now I am much wiser
Next time before I bask
I will be very careful
To look for Ministry behind the mask.

Money has a Voice

I want to tell you something
Money has a voice
It cries out to be noticed
"Pick ME as your first choice"
It doesn't want you to live free
It wants to bind you up
"Fall in love with ME" it cries
"And I will fill your cup"
"With riches and position,
I will take you far
Your house, your job, material things
You must have THE best car"
Don't get me wrong these things aren't bad
In life you need such means
But to fall in love with mammon
It's sadder than it seems
What does it profit a man in life
If he loses his own soul
No amount of worldly things
Will fill and make you whole
God wants to be your first-place
Deep within your heart
Don't surround yourself with riches
And live your life apart
From God who actually owns it all
It's not yours anyway
He created everything
And blesses us each day
It's not a sin to have nice stuff
Just don't make it number one
Enjoy the things God gives you
He wants you to have fun

But money it will always shout
And entice you with its voice
Just remember not to bow to it
And make God your first-love choice!

Morning Love Poem

You are my God
You are my King
You are the reason that I sing
Every morning when I awake
Every gift my hands do make
I will arise above the dark
And in this world
I will make my mark
Declaring of your wonderous love
That you have sent down from Heaven above
His name is Jesus
Can't you see Him?
His name is Jesus
Can't you feel Him?
His name is Jesus
Do you know Him?
The King of kings
And Lord of lords
Let us praise Him
In one accord
He is returning one day soon
On a white horse
And for some it's doom
Don't let that be you!
Be His child
Let your heart be meek and mild
And seek Him high
And seek Him low
For His glorious love
It is worth to know
His love will take you
Above the clouds
His love will snatch you

From the crowds
You will be His chosen one
And His love will leave you
Immensely undone
So, make Jesus your God
Make Jesus your King
Make Jesus the reason
You rise and sing
And I can guarantee
You will never be the same
He will wash away
Your sin and your shame
A new life Jesus will give to you
And then your heart will be changed too
Life with Jesus
Is the BEST
Just open your heart
And God will do the rest!

Morning Song

SING THIS TO THE LORD WITH YOUR OWN TUNE

God of all Creation
Fill my life today

Lead me with your Presence
Come by my side and stay

CHORUS
Oh, my Lord I long for you
As I start my day
Oh, my Lord, I cry to you
Teach me all your ways

Let me show the world your love
By living in your word

Then others too will see you
The ones who've never heard

CHORUS
Oh, my Lord I long for you
As I start my day
Oh, my Lord, I cry to you
Teach me all your ways

When I'm full of wisdom
And my hair is grey

I will love you more my Lord
For in MY heart, you'll stay

CHORUS
Oh, my Lord I long for you
As I start my day
Oh, my Lord, I cry to you
Teach me all your ways

CHORUS
Oh, my Lord I long for you
As I start my day
Oh, my Lord I long for you
Come fill my life today.

My Bible

I love to read my Bible, Lord
And gaze upon your word
You tell me that no eye has seen
Nor has any ear heard
Of all the wonderful promises
That you have in store for me
That in the pages of this book
Are miracles and victories
I need to feed upon it
Every single day
It's bread and water to my soul
A lamp to guide my way
Every time I read it
There's always something new
The Holy Spirit's power
Revealing what He'll do
God is everywhere at once
He is all-powerful
He knows the beginning and the end
Now this is beautiful
There is no other God like you
None found upon this earth
No other God was conceived
By a virgin birth
And came and walked among the crowds
Your son you gave to us
Jesus was a man and God
And died upon a cross
To take away our sin so deep
And speak forth truth and love
To tell us of your mansions
You have in heaven above
How do I know these wonders

That I'm sharing now?
I read them in my Bible
The who and what and how
I invite you to the table
To dine with the Great King
And feast upon HIS WRITTEN WORD
Pure life for everything
So, come and read God's love for you
Recorded from the ages
You will find they are His love letters
Written in the pages
And as you read God's promises
That are there for you and me
The Holy Spirit will respond to you
With miracles that set you free!

My Call

God is preparing the way for me
To journey on this road
And when it gets too heavy
He will help me with my load
Sometimes, I feel like I am lost
Where am I going Lord?
He has a plan that is so great
Because I am adored
AND loved – AND cherished – God loves me so
My seasons are all worth it
So, today I will surrender all
And tomorrow I will live it
No matter where God has me
On the stage or in the cave
I will love HIM with all my heart
That's how I will behave
God wants to test what's in my heart
And how I live again
Do I choose to walk with God
Or for the praise of men
God gives, He takes and then He breaks
When He gives MY CALL
He wants to see what I will do
Will I give my all?
He puts me in the furnace
It's hot and I do cry
It's so the gold in me will rise
I'm not to question why?
It is ALL for a reason
Why God must deal with me
So, I can daily overcome
And live in VICTORY!

My Child

One day a babe was born
And taken without a trace
Her mother never held her
Nor gazed upon her face
She hoped one day to know her baby
And who she'd grow to be
And prayed she would survive the world
To fulfil her destiny
One thing would never leave her
Though their lives were torn apart
"You will always be MY CHILD -
You will live inside my heart".

The new adoptive parents were
As happy as can be
They have a baby daughter
To complete their family
They had all the love to give her
Her little room a special place
And every day they'd wake to see
The smile upon her face
This love would never leave them
It was given to their heart
"You will always be MY CHILD –
Even when we are apart".

As the child grew tall and strong
Surrounded by love and care
God watched over her in perfect love
Though she was not aware
"I have your life marked out for you
Your road already planned
You don't even know me yet
But your life is in my hand
There is one thing that you should know
As you search inside your heart
You are also MY CHILD as well
And we will never part".

MY CHILD was where everything started.
I wrote this poem the day I lost everything.
My husband was a Pastor in Ministry and his fall in our
Church caused the loss of everything that goes with
exposure to marital unfaithfulness.
Overnight I lost my marriage.
My ministry. My home. My finances.
My possessions. My dream. My Identity.
March 1995 to be exact.
Broken and devastated I struggled to understand
who I was after such a loss.
I lay on my bed, my tears saturating the pillow,
and cried out to God.
"WHO AM I NOW IN THIS WORLD AND WHAT AM I TO DO?"
God spoke clearly into my spirit,
"YOU ARE MY CHILD".
This truth gave me comfort.
That's ALL I had to be for right now! HIS child!
...and with that revelation deep inside me the
words flowed out.

I was my birth mother's child. I was my adoptive mother's child.
I was God's child. This poem made up my identity!
And then God spoke again and said,
"IT WILL BE A BOOK ONE DAY".
In disbelief, I held God to His promise and 25 years later
this poem became
MY CHILD AND THE TAPESTRY OF LIFE
– A Destiny Woven for Victory!
A woman's journey to heal the little girl inside.
(My personal and raw journey to healing
mental health and trauma).
After this, I created evangelistic jewellery called WOVEN.
Then a Ministry called Heart Weaves was formed.
A team of women gathered around me,
and we became Heart Weavers.
A trauma healing workshop was established
and together we serve and teach women tools
to navigate their trauma healing.

Never underestimate how God wants
to lead you into your destiny.
It could be a small simple poem
but given into the Master's hand...
Well, just see what He can do!

My Shepherd

Lord, you are my Shepherd
And I shall never want
Your pastures green I do lie down
Quiet waters from the font
My soul, you do restore me
And guide my every step
Along the paths of righteousness
You haven't failed me yet
For your name's sake, there's safety
And even though I stray
Or find myself in valleys
You're with me all the way
Because death it cannot touch me
It is only but a shadow
I fear no evil at any time
For you're my God, I do know
Your rod and staff they comfort me
And a table you've prepared
Before my every enemy
But I will not be scared
My head you do anoint with oil
And my cup it overflows
Surely goodness and your mercy
Follow me wherever I go
And one day I will be with you
In eternity we will share
The love of God forevermore
With my Shepherd who will be there.

My Special Friend

Friends they come and friends they go
Why this happens, I don't know
Some end in laughter, some end in tears
I've had many friends through the years
Some have taken, some they gave
I could not change the way they'd behave
Some brought joy, some brought pain
And some I've never seen again
I have one special friend in life
One I've had for years
He's seen me laugh
He's seen my cry
He knows my deepest fears
He understands me when I'm cross
And does not rush away
He comes to comfort me when I'm sad
And by my side, He'll stay
He never is too busy
For me at any time
Day or night or morning
Anytime with Him is fine
He cares when I am worried
About something big or small
He never thinks I'm silly
And never lets me fall
His arms of friendship always reach
A lot longer than mine do back
I know I've hurt him in the past
And my heart does sometimes lack
But that does not change His love for me
Wherever I may go
Even when I am alone
His love for me I know

I am so very lucky
To have a friend so rare
To have a friend who has such faith
In me and really cares
My friend is very wonderful
And Jesus is His name
I called his name out loud one day
And in my heart, He came
You see, my friend is very special
And there's nothing He can't do
If you call His name out loud
He will be your SPECIAL FRIEND too.

Never Leave or Forsake

There is a promise in the Bible
Open it and see
Jesus will speak into your heart
It is for you and me
The words declare a promise
That He will never break
Whatever path you take in life
Whatever plans you make
He will never leave you
Or ever will forsake
But follow right behind you
Make no mistake!
That God's love is Agape
That means He has no strings
He doesn't manipulate you
Or bribe you with many things
Because His love is oh so pure
And His promises are true
And this one is very special
To never leave or forsake YOU!

No more Lust

There is a sin that needs God's light
To shine amidst the dark
No one likes to speak such things
So, they live with this black mark
But God wants us to be open
To His healing touch this day
And if this sin's a problem
Then God will take it away
No need to live in bondage and shame
Expose the hidden thing
Let's talk about this sin right now
So that your soul can sing
The devil circles some with lust
He traps them with this vice
But the Bible shows us how to live
Let's look at this advice
Stay away from seductive eyes
They will always lure you in
They have only one agenda
To drag you into sin
Stay away from getting drunk
Lust uses this strategy
To make you intoxicated
So, you never will be free
Stay away from watching porn
Yes, I said it – let's be real
Make the choice deep in your soul
Turn away from how you feel
Stay away from evil predators
Who lure and plan and dream
Pray for their exposure
End their disgusting schemes
Come on Christian – let's rise up

We can defeat this foe
And bring the world to purity
To a God they need to know
He will unchain their strongholds
They will be bound no more
Set free to live in holiness
And righteous to their core
So, if you need such freedom
From this sin of lust
Repent and pray this prayer out loud -

*"God, with you my life I trust
Take all that is within me
That binds me in the dark
And rid me of this bondage
That makes my life so stark
I do not want this anymore
Take this sin away
And come and wash me white as snow
Live in me today
And make me pure and holy
No more lust is in my heart
My eyes they only gaze on you
Thank you for my brand-new start
Help me speak and change the world
In this subject that's taboo
And bring others now to freedom
In what they say and do
And make this world a better place
Of love and purity
And live in peace and holiness
With our God who sets us free."*

No more Mountains

I've been around this mountain
Time and time again
I do not see I'm doing it
The what – the why – the when
You see, I'm blinded by my own will
Striving to be free
I want it to go my way
I want my life to be
Just how 'I' do see it
And what 'I' think is best
Round and round and round I go
Never to find my rest
And God allows this in my life
He's testing me you know
Watching down with loving eyes
Seeing which way I'll go
It's my way or the highway
I've planned each step I take
This is what 'I' want God
Come on! Give me a break!
I think I know what I need
So, I tell God what that is
The truth is that He knows what's best
The what – the that – the this
His will is what my heart should seek
God, what is it YOU say?
About my life, my health, my joy
My blessings every day
Surrender is what I should do
Surrender everything
Take 'me' off my heart's throne
And place YOU there as King
Then my life will make sense

And I will have great peace
And going round my mountain
Will finally end and cease
And you will give me answers
To my lifelong cry
I will come to understand
The what – the where – the why
I'm glad I've finally surrendered
To your Sovereign will for me
And while I didn't understand
Your path now sets me free
No more this mountain in my life
For me to go around
Because in YOUR great will for me
Finally, peace I've found.

No More Questions

God says that in the last days
There will be a strong delusion
In the hearts and minds of many
Life will be a false illusion
Of what they want to think and do
Nothing is off the table
There will be confusion and chaos
Nowhere will be stable
Wars and earthquakes, fires and floods
It's prophesied in God's word
Life will be terrifying
Like you've never seen or heard
But yes! – there is a Saviour
A rescuer for your soul
The only way to freedom
And for you to be made whole
In your mind and body
Jesus will set you free
No more questions in your mind
No more doubts of victory
So, trust in a God who brings the light
Into the darkest place
And your heart will be in total peace
Because you have seen HIS face.

Parents, please......

Train me up in the Lord
When I'm innocent
And when I grow up in years
I will be obedient
You see – taking out the Lord's prayer
When I go to school
Will take away a strong faith
That is my life-long tool
And if you let me answer back
When you discipline me
I will have no respect for others
And selfish I will be
And don't take Jesus out of Christmas
Christ's birth He is the reason
God gave us Jesus as our gift
To celebrate Him this season
Guide me in God's morals
And in His Holiness
So, when I make life choices
They are full with much goodness
And keep my heart and mind
On life's steady road
And I will be very happy
As God's peace daily flows
And Jesus will be my faithful friend
Who never leaves my side
See why this is important
To teach me in your stride?
So don't neglect the Bible
To teach it in my day
For then when I am older
My life is blessed this way

God will send His blessings
Around me yes, it's true
So, parents never ever stop
Sharing God in all I do.

Perfect in God

I do not have to be perfect
For God to love me so
He holds no sin against me
When I come and bow down low
And ask for His forgiveness
He casts it into the sea
God forgets my sins forever
If it's remembered -
Well...that's on me
If I could count every grain of sand
Which is impossible to do
Whatever is the number
God's love is that times two
His love is more than all the sand
Counted on the shore
It's hard to get my head around
Just how much I'm adored
But I'm thankful every day to God
For His love and His salvation
Now I want the world to know
His love for every nation
And tribe and tongue that's ever lived
Jesus died for all
The old, the young, the wise, the not
The children, oh so small
So come to God just as you are
Still your heart and then reflect
That it's only through the love of God
That you will be perfect.

Power and Glory

I wrote my story years ago
I knew it was my call
God wanted me to share it
And tell it to you all
Of why and what and where and who
Impacted on my life
Some chapters they are full of love
And others' deep dark strife
But one thing that is woven
Through my heartfelt story
Is God's never-ending love
In all His Power and Glory
God's love always surrounded me
I'm protected by His hand
And though I've felt much anguish
His love has made me stand
Strong and true – forever hopeful
His blue-print plan for me
I will never turn away from God
He is my Victory
I hold His hand when things are fine
And also when it's tough
Through valleys and the mountain tops
When life is joyful or rough
Whatever is my season
God wants me just to trust
And even though I don't understand
Having faith is a certain must
So, journey with me - come and read
Find hope for your life too
And God will take your hand I know
And prove what He can do
He'll take away your pain and sorrow

Restore your broken heart
He'll fill you with love and wholeness
Let His Spirit do His part
To re-write some of your pages
Like He did for me
For you to tell your story
For all the world to see
That God is a Master Weaver
He has threads to weave in you
Replace all of your dark strands
With gold colours that are new
And full of life and blessings
To re-write your own story
And just like God has done for me
Heal you with Power and Glory!

Pray for Israel

I feel your heartbreak God every day
For all the people who've lost their way
Violence and evil were never your plan
But these arise from the works of man
Who have never met the one true God
And some say Jesus is damned and odd
But He is the one you sent to earth
To give our hearts a love-filled birth
The grace of Heaven and all things good
Yes, the Bible is misunderstood
Because ISRAEL is the apple of your eye
And you don't want anyone to die
In senseless wars and evil attacks
Where those in the streets must watch their backs
Because of evil men who want to kill
Innocent lives on your HOLY HILL
We PRAY FOR ISRAEL
To have much PEACE
That soon this war will completely cease
And your judgements will be just and fair
WE CALL FOR PEACE,
WE SHOUT AND DECLARE!
O come, Lord Jesus! Come and deal
With those whose hearts have an evil seal
And deliver your people once again
Set them all free from these evil men
We hold on in hope to our God of great Power
We seek your face in this day and hour
To save Jerusalem one more time
Because you say – ISRAEL IS MINE!

2023 ... with love and standing with Israel.

Prayer

There are many ways to talk to God
Enjoying Heaven's dew
Try them in your daily life
And these are just a few
I come and sit before God's Throne
And magnify His name
First thing every morning
God will love it that you came
Then I put my music on
And dance around in praise
Who cares about the neighbours
My hands I fully raise
Or I take my worship flags
And wave them in the air
Holy Spirit flows with me
I surrender without a care
Then I get my Bible out
And feast upon God's word
He shows me secret treasures
No eye has seen or heard
Or I can pray in my spiritual tongue
It is God's gift to me
I edify my spirit
And declare my Victories!
Maybe a gentle whisper
At night upon my bed
God even knows my heart-thoughts
Before one of them is said
So, I'll stay connected to my Lord
All throughout my day
He doesn't care how you talk to Him
Just make sure that you pray.

Prosperity

God wants your life to prosper
In each and every way
With money, health and wisdom
Every single day
It's when you go a little off-track
And focus on one thing
This is called obsession
When to one thing you do cling
It then becomes an idol
And consumes your everyday
Your thoughts, your words, your deeds
Are challenged in this way
Obsession does not prosper
When it doesn't come from God
God will not bless your cravings
He will not bow and nod
And give His very best blessing
He will not honour lust
God wants your heart-felt focus
On Him to always trust
So, yes God wants you to be blessed
With great prosperity
Just don't make things your idols
They'll stop you from living free
Trust in the Lord with all your heart
Lean not on your own understanding
And God will come through in all you do
When life becomes demanding
If you make God your number one
And seek just only HE
Then money, health and wisdom
Will be your prosperity.

Purity

Come wash your garments
Of sin and stain
Let my Holy Spirit
Make you white again
For some, you have chosen
An idol of desire
You have not read my word
Or done what I require
My grace has covered you
In your walk thus far
But sin has entered
And your door is ajar
It's time to love me
First in your life
And put to death
All the sinful strife
The taste in my mouth
I can stand it no more
My son died for you
Do I have to say "What for?"
The love I have for you
Is Holy and pure
Why do you choose sin?
And take satan's lure?
Warning after warning
I have given to be fair
ENOUGH IS ENOUGH
I am sifting the tare
Cry out to me
Before it's too late
When my Holy judgement
Will bring down sin's fate
I love you, my Bride

But you must be in white
Because when I come
I will come when it's night
So be ready and surrendered
Give heed to my cry
For I love you, my child
You're the apple of my eye.

Safe in My Father's Hand

There is a place I often go
A place of safety that I know
When I am lonely or deep in fear
This place is very, very near
You cannot see it with your eye
But it is vast
It's as large as the sky
Full of love and warmth and peace
Ever flowing and will never cease
I close my eyes and it's dark and dim
I take a breath and run into HIM
Right into the place that's made for me
My senses are full – no need to see
And there I sit so still and safe
There is nothing like
This incredible place
My God, my Father –
This is where you planned
For me to be safe
In your magnificent hand.

Stay in your own Lane

God is calling you to serve Him
Deep within your heart
Pressing you with His Great Love
To come and be a part
Of His Kingdom service
Dressed in humility
Wearing a pure garment
Of spirituality
God will train your hands
Your feet He will lead too
He'll place others on your path
To help you with all you do
So, when God starts to open doors
One thing I will suggest
This is so important
For you to be your best
Don't seek approval from others
That only comes from God
Just fix your eyes on Jesus
When others say you're odd
Don't look to the left or to the right
Don't seek fan-fare or great fame
Just listen and obey your Father's will
And stay in your own lane
Then you will accomplish much
In service, you will be
A leader in God's army
With many Victories
I will repeat myself again
Don't seek fan-fare or great fame
It's imperative to remember
To stay in your own lane!

Surrendered at your Feet

My beautiful Lord – here I am
Sitting at your feet
It's where I come to be with you
It's here where we do meet
I pour out all my worship
Adoration, thanks and praise
I will sing to you a new song
Your love will fill my days
I do not come to get from you
I come to surrender and give
You are the longing of my heart
The reason why I live
Worship tears flow for you
In wonder and in awe
You are my peace, my joy, my strength
And then you're so much more
I give you my life, I say here I am
Send me where your heart will guide
And I will go and share your love
With you always by my side
I love you, Lord, you give me life
For all eternity
You took my sin, my pain, my darkness
And truly set me free
So, I sit at your feet and pour out my love
It's okay if no one understands
But I pray one day they absolutely will
Put their life into your hands
And they will find this same love
The day when you both meet
And take their place to worship you
Surrendered at your feet.

Taste and See

Taste and see that the Lord is good
Come now one and all
Can you hear God calling you
Harken to His call
Don't delay just come right now
The table is set for you
And delight in all God's goodness
His love for you is true
Jesus is just Oh, so sweet
Let His Spirit marinate
Your heart, your mind, your body
Just drink all you can take
As you feast daily on God's word
It will change your life inside
God will reveal His love for you
So deep, so high, so wide
Will you accept God's invitation?
For this banquet meal
The menu is the Bible
His word is very real
So come and sup and linger
Don't eat and run away
But savour every mouthful
And be full in God all day.

Thank you for my Healing

I've prayed to God for healing
Deep within my soul
My past has damaged my body
And I scream to be made whole
To do that I must surrender
According to God's plan
And leave the healing up to Him
I want to understand
As God leads me on this journey
Over many years
Through mountains and dark valleys
Through highs and many tears
I'm told I have no faith by some
If I'm not instantly healed
That really is an awful thing
My fate which they have sealed
But through the valleys and the hills
My faith's been tested there
And even though my journey's long
God tells me that He cares
And goes before my every step
To pave the healing way
Who can predict God's methods
If I'm healed at the end of the day?
Operations, therapy, vitamins and meds
It's all the same to Him
God's given us great Doctors
They are trained and skilled to win
So, I'll trust God's guidance for my life
And not question as He leads
For through God's perfect avenue
He will meet my every need
A healing is God's healing

Whichever way it comes
A miracle or medicine
A holiday in the sun
Lead me, Lord I am all yours
And surrendered to your dealing
Whichever way it comes to me
I thank you for my healing.

The Beginning of Easter
THROUGH THE EYES OF MARY MAGDELENE

JESUS! JESUS! No! What have they done?
Don't they know He IS God's son
How can they kill Him and nail Him to that cross
They don't know what they're doing
They don't know WHO they've lost!
God sent Him to earth
YOU ARE JESUS, the Saviour
You be-friended and delivered us
From our sinful behaviour
You shared the secrets of Heaven
And showed us God's love
And now...you are dying on the cross high above
For all the world to see!
Why are you cheering?
You don't know what his life meant to me!
Jesus, your hands, your feet, your face
I can hardly recognise you, Lord
There is so much blood
Oh! This is a disgrace!
They've torn into your flesh
They've ripped your side apart
OH, LORD! MY LORD! I give you my heart!
Jesus, Jesus, what did you say?
Now it is finished, you must go away.
Oh Lord, everything is dark, there is no sun,
This is so frightening,
They are shouting they've won!
I must go quickly, let me through, give me room
I'm going to mourn at my Lord's prepared tomb
Jesus lies in there, He's wrapped all in white
I'll bring you spices and perfume
In three days when it's light
The stone so large has now rolled in place

Oh Lord, I'm grieving, already I miss your face…
One day, two days, three days passed
Mary with her friends arrived back at last
To a tomb that was empty, eerie and cold
Two angels appeared saying,
"HE's RISEN" as foretold
Filled with joy, though a little afraid
The women set off to Galilee
Where the disciples had stayed
Suddenly, Jesus appeared
With glad tiding and greeting
Mary fell at His feet in worship at their meeting
Jesus spoke with a message full of LOVE…

What I say to you now is from my Father above
Mary, Mary, go spread the word
Tell my disciples what you have seen and heard
Say that you've met ME
And surely I have risen
Tell them Mary their sins are 'still' forgiven
For I have yet to go to my Father's right-hand
Mary, my dying and rising was part of God's plan
For those who love me, for those who believe
My resurrected Spirit they shall also receive
NO! You won't see my body, my flesh must depart
But, my Spirit, the Comforter will abide in your heart
For now and forever I will be your LORD
Learn my ways, rise up in my Spirit,
My word is your sword
I hand you my power, my Spirit is free
I will give it to ALL who dare to follow me
Nothing can harm you, and no darkness can win
Because in my RISING, you have VICTORY over sin!
Mary, I now live forever and because of this day
Every Christian who dies
Will be resurrected the same way
To live with my Father and see ME face to face
Mary, have hope, here is a portion of my GRACE

My Lord, this day will be remembered year after year
We have reason to grieve, yet have reason to cheer
May your death and life be a festive season to celebrate
May God's love be made known in a word full of hate
Even though I will miss you, Jesus you must rise in the sky
And we will proclaim that YOUR LOVE will NEVER die
For you are the TRUTH the LIFE and the WAY
And EASTER will be celebrated
– BECAUSE OF THIS DAY!

The Broad & Narrow Road

We are all born on the broad road
In this thing called life
Let me tell you about this road
That all it holds is strife
Sin at every signpost
Directing you the way
Satan and his demons
Enticing you to play
With things God says we must never touch
To entertain our flesh
Black and white now merge together
This road is a grey-coloured mesh
I do what I want and I say what I think
My life it has no conscience
I follow blindly these road signs
My life is full of nonsense
But off to the side of this broad road
I see a narrow one
It's small and humble and full of love
And calls me just to - COME
Come and see what this road is
It's different I must say
Full of light and gentleness
No strife is on this way
Then I see Him standing there
Jesus your PEACE I feel
With arms open wide He comes to me
This is just SO REAL!
His love it does envelop me
And washes away my sin
All that I was born with
From my outside and within
Please forgive me OH MY LORD

Thank you for dying for me
It WAS for a specific purpose
Your death would set me FREE!
And take me off this broad road
That my soul was born onto
And place my spirit in Heavenly realms
My life now starts anew
We all have the choice of choosing
Which road we will walk upon
The broad road full of lust and sin
Or the narrow road along
Satan has no hold on you
Throw his roadbook far away
And read the guide that God has made
HIS WORD in full display
It's written in the Bible
And it's TRUTH for you and me
To live each step firm on God's love
Good news and VICTORY!
So, make the turn and leave the street
Where TURMOIL is the sign
And find the narrow path in life
Where Jesus says - "YOU'RE MINE"
I can guarantee it's worth it
It's a choice you won't regret
And in time all of that darkness
You will very soon forget
And live on paths of righteousness
Mercy, goodness and God's grace
And every signpost you will see
Will shine down on your face
No more dark paths my feet will tread
No more sickness, loss or strife
Because the narrow path that I now walk
Is FULL of LOVE AND LIFE

The Good News

If you turn the TV on
At 5 o'clock each day
You'll hear a news reporter
Speak to us as they relay
About stabbings, deaths and fires
And con-men on the run
About wars over religion
And a world that's coming undone
Disaster after disaster
We are told it every day
They fill our lives with many words
Which cause us to be afraid
Is there any good news
Where I can live a life
With hope and peace and so much joy
And live without this strife?
Well yes – I am so very glad
You've asked me this today
For I know that there IS good news
So, hear me when I say
God sent His own son Jesus
As a gift to you and me
Just believe He is the son of God
And your life will be set free
You'll live in a different Kingdom
In the spiritual sense, I mean
Where angels live and follow you
Your life is now redeemed
From all the bad things in the world
They cannot do you harm
For God sends angel armies
No more to be alarmed

Of all the bad news in the world
The GOOD NEWS is here today
And His name is JESUS
Forever in our hearts to stay!

The Mystery of Love

Some say love is one big mystery
But it's not until you know it's history
That you understand how love came to be
In this world for you and me
Love began in God's own heart
He wants us all to be a part
Of this great thing that He calls love
That He sent down from Heaven above
For God so loved the world and you
His love sent Jesus to love you too
And Jesus showed us God's pure plan
For every woman and every man
Love is what we are searching for
And when we find it, we want more
Because love is patient and consistently kind
It's unconditional love we long to find
It's not jealous or rude or says it's your fault
But it's gracious and honest and seasoned with salt
It is not self-seeking or boastful or proud
It doesn't give up – no that's not allowed
Love never stops loving or ever fades away
Love wakes every morning with your fill for today
We are all in search of this Great Love
Sent as a gift from Heaven above
So, when you find love hold it dear
Treasure it daily and keep it near
Do all you can to keep love alive
Cherish it always so it will thrive
Whether God, animals, family or a friend
Your journey of love will never end
And if you find 'your one true' mate
Then it's blessed by Heaven – a beautiful fate.

The One
DEDICATED TO JESS

Jesus left the 99
And went after the one
Held and trapped in darkness
This lamb had been undone
Somewhere in its fragile life
It was led astray
Many harsh distractions
Came into their day
This lamb was me when I was young
So innocent and naive
I didn't see the pitfalls
That were in front of me

Look to the left and to the right
I have some greener grass
Many things to tempt you
Anything you ask
I can give you whatever you want
A dark voice tempted me

Leading into deception
It didn't want me to be free
And then quite out of nowhere
Loving arms, they held me tight
It was my faithful Shepherd
I was His only delight
He told me that He loved me
And His green pasture was just fine
That He died so I can live with Him
He said, CHILD YOU ARE MINE

No more will I stray again
Close by His feet, I'll stay
Thank you, Jesus, for leaving the 99
I was your ONE that day.

The Power of God's Word

Do you know your words have power?
In the atmosphere
Speak them loudly as you claim
And a shift will soon appear
*No, it is not magic
That is quite absurd
It is the Power of Almighty God
The Power of HIS WORD*
In the beginning, God did say
To the dark, "Let there be light"
And immediately He created
An essence oh-so-bright
Everything was established
By the Power of God's word
The trees, the rivers, the sun and moon
Mountains, flowers and every bird
*No, it is not magic
That is quite absurd
It is the Power of Almighty God
The Power of HIS WORD*
Then God spoke into the dirt
And a man was formed
Then from man came woman
And both God did adore
God told them that He loved them
And gave them a special gift
That they can speak words from their mouth
The atmosphere to shift
*No, it is not magic
That is quite absurd
It is the Power of Almighty God
The Power of HIS WORD*
But we are not a big God
Just favoured on this earth

And from God's hand of love to us
We can have new birth
To speak out words of power
To renounce all of our sin
To acknowledge Jesus as our Lord
His Spirit to live within
Now we can daily declare God's will
In the Power of HIS NAME
Speaking Jesus Christ is Lord
We will never be the same
What a gift God's given us
To daily speak His word
I declare it to the atmosphere
To Heaven, it is heard
No, it is not magic
That is quite absurd
It is the Power of Almighty God
The Power of HIS WORD.

The Promise is Coming

There is coming a time
There is coming a place
Where you will see your promise
Face to face
You will have to wait
You will have to pray
You will have to give thanks
Until that fate-filled day
There is nothing you can do
There is nothing you can say
That will stop or bring sooner
God's promise your way
But wait looking up
Looking up at the sky
Giving thanks every day
As the moments pass by
Do not be anxious
Do not shed a tear
Do not sit around
Consumed by fear
Be as free as the eagle
Rise with strength and power
And surely you will see
When it comes at the hour
Your heart will not doubt
You will finally see
All your plans and your dreams
They have come to be
So be happy my child
For the walk on the way
Rejoice and be glad
For the things of today

For the promise is coming
And it shall be soon
For the promise it's happening
So don't be all doom
You are loved, my child
Be content and free
God's timing is perfect
... just wait and see!

The Truth

The truth it will come out in time
And expose the lies that were told
God will eventually clear your name
When your character was sold
By those who were a Judas
They kissed your cheek and smiled
But they chose their own agenda
And your life they left defiled
Of course, this really is not nice
To have this done to you
That others twist and turn and say
Your good deeds are not true
But God knows what is actually right
He sees deep in your heart
Who cares what others do believe
It's been error from the start
God is your defender
And justice HE will bring
Just keep your focus and your prayers
To Him – your soul will sing
And bless all those who curse you
They know not what they do
It's just a shame they are deceived
Lord – set their lives free too
One thing about deception
You see the black as white
You see the lie as if it's truth
And what is wrong is right
But one day God will reveal and bring
The truth into the light
And all the lies and chatter
Will run away with fright

At the power of God's Glory
He is VICTOR of it all
He is your true defender
He'll make you stand up tall
And fulfil your call and destiny
To His excellent detail
Understand in the word of God
You're the head and not the tail
I could write another book
How satan's tried to stop me
But every time he's tried his tricks
God brings me into VICTORY
So, if you hear any whispers
About me I would say
Come to me directly
Be quick and don't delay
Hear both sides of the story
And then make up your mind
And see if what they're saying
Is true or just unkind
But one thing is for certain
If they mistrust your words or mine
That God will shine His light down
And the truth will come out in time.

The Well

Thirsty and dry I trudged the hill
To the well to quench my thirst
To my surprise, a man was there
My heart did swell and burst
Jesus had gone before me
And had waited at the well
It was His love that took Him there
To end my life of hell
I was darkened with much sin
Many men had scarred my heart
I was broken, lost and sad
For these – I played my part
I felt His love when he softly spoke
So kind, so pure, so true
No judgment for my sins of lust
I could not hide – He knew!
Of all the ones who hurt me so
His love was there to bind
And quench my thirst with water pure
His essence I did find
His living water for my soul
It washed my sins away
He did not leave me like the rest
But by my side, He stayed
He said His name was Jesus
Full of living water
And washed me clean, my spirit filled
I am God's chosen daughter
So, now I have some news to share
That I found there at the well
Jesus' love is water pure
For me to find and tell.

The Words of a Prayer

Words are sometimes so unfair
Filled with such an emptiness
Words are full of hate and pain
Lead deeper into darkness.
Does anybody out there, care?
Some words are never carried through -
Broken promises, lies - hide and cheat
And finally shatter the light in the world
What word will you speak to show you care?
I've heard them all before...
Silent are the words that live in a loving heart
Often you can see these words in a caring eye
They have no sound
You can feel the words in the air
As they come and surround you like an army
They give you comfort and strength
Bringing peace where there was none before
Pushing away the darkness and healing a broken heart
From a life so unfair, now there is joy
My life has turned around to find a treasure of hope!
But where did it come from?
I didn't hear one word!
Somebody out there does care!
The words are so simple, yet powerful
They are the loving words of an
Uncondional Prayer...

Three-fold Cord

I am a 2-fold cord
With my God above
And though we're strong together
Sometimes, it's not enough
You see, being a single person
Has benefits that is true
But when you are totally on your own
There's a lot you cannot do
Like fixing taps and faucets
And climbing on the roof
Working out life's answers
Being a super sleuth
You get it right - you get it wrong
There's no one to confide
With all your deepest worries
No one by your side
Don't get me wrong I do have God
And together we're a team
But keeping warm and getting up
Is harder than it seems
So even though I'm happy
With just my God and me
To have a life-long partner
Would complete my victories
Have mercy on the single one
God grant me my other cord
And together we'll entwine our lives
And forever Praise the Lord!

Time

I somehow miss the old days
When life was nice and slow
How things have changed over the years
Where has time gone? – I don't know!
It only feels like yesterday
That my children were oh so small
Now when they stand next to me
They are very, very tall
One thing that life has taught me
Over the past years
That time is short and precious
Through laughter, fun and tears
So, find out what's important
For your life today
And do the very thing you love
No excuses or delay
Because God has given you this life
To give and to receive
Answered prayers and miracles
For those who do believe
So, as the clock does tick away
Live life and make it shine
Be grateful for life's many things
With our precious God-blessed time.

Traffic Lights

God taught me how to wait on Him
With a method that's just right
I'll share my secret strategy
And I call it 'Traffic Lights'
Red means stop and green means go
And amber, well – that's wait
I see them with my spiritual eye
So, I'm never early or late
When I see the red light
After I have prayed
I never go or move ahead
In obedience, I will stay
And when I see the amber
Shining back at me
It means I wait and do not move
Great patience I do need
But finally - when God knows best
The light I see is green
I move out boldly on His command
And trust that what I've seen
Is His very will for me
I venture calm and slow
God directs my traffic lights
His perfect plan I know
So, if you're having trouble
Knowing which way to go
Ask God for your own lights
And ask Him then to show
When the lights change colour
From amber, red or green
You'll then be in God's perfect plan
And prayer is easier than it seems.

Treasures in Heaven
DEDICATED TO JILL

God has treasures in Heaven
Waiting just for you
Come sit before His throne of Grace
That's all you have to do
And as you wait and search God's heart
He'll share His word with you
And speak wonderful promises
His love is pure and true
Take His hand and let Him lead
Deeper and deeper you'll go
Abiding with Holy Spirit
In Heaven's realm, you'll flow
Mysteries beyond mysteries
Spoken to your heart
God will show you His Glory
And this is just the start
As you'll find His word is real
To your very being
God will infuse Himself with you
Beyond the realm of seeing
So many spiritual riches
Prepared only for you
Heaven's Design and tailor-made
The table is set for two
So come and dine with Jesus
You can never get enough
And partake of God's treasures
And the delicacies of His love.

Waiting on God

Waiting on God is not easy
For the promise He gave you within
Day after day your patience is tried
It's a wrestle to not be in sin
You see – having a tantrum will do you no good
I've had a few in the wait
Tears and whining and stamping my feet
In the fear that God has been late

I've shouted…

"GOD! You have forgotten me!
And it's proof that you don't care!
You keep me in this silent prison
I'm trapped, it's just not fair!
You download all these promises
And confirm them in your word
And then nothing at all happens
REALLY? This is just SO absurd!"

But then - a miracle happens!
Deep within my soul
The wait IS for a reason
So, YOU can make ME whole
Whole in faith and endurance
You want character in me
You shape and mould and temper
My gold for all to see
That you're a God of love and truth
And you'll bring the victory!
But it's IN the wait and suffering
That my promise will definitely…
Be perfect in YOUR timing

You will do just so much more
Blessing upon blessing
Is what you have in store
So – help me in the wait Lord
And put me to the test
And I shall gladly sit in peace
And wait for your very best!

Walking in the footsteps of my Love

Walk with me
Talk with me
I am leading you
Into great things
Walk with me
Talk with me
I am showing you
What My Love brings
For as you have waited
As you have prayed
You will soon see
The destiny I have paved
One of splendour
One of grace
One that reflects
My shining face
GLORY! GLORY!
Is all about
So weighty and pure
You will praise and shout
That all my promises
Have come to pass
You have now received
Because you have asked!
Your steps are steady
And led from above
As you walked daily
In the footsteps of My Love
So, rejoice my daughter
And sing a new song
Sing of where you
Desire to belong
In my presence

My heart for you
Overflows with
Heaven's dew
You have kept the faith
And not given up
So now you will drink
From Victory's Cup
Walk with me
Talk with me
About every
Great thing
Walk with me
Talk with me
Let your
Heart sing
Follow me always
My Holy Spirit dove
Your heart forever trusting
In the footsteps of My Love.

Warrior Princess

I am a Warrior Princess
Trained deep in my soul
It's taken many, many years
With practice to be whole
Skilled in spiritual warfare
Most done on bended knee
Fighting demons and witchcraft
Setting the captives free
God downloads special intel
Straight from Heaven's realm
Through visions and prophetic dreams
Sometimes, I'm overwhelmed
At the schemes and wiles of satan
He's evil at his best
His plans are pure destruction
To your life, he brings no rest
He is the deliverer of all things bad
And harmful in every way
He robs, he kills, he does destroy
If you try to thwart his day
But God has way more power
And an army He is training
That's you and me, the new recruits
We have God's power just by reigning
Joined with God in spiritual places
We take our shield and sword
And pull down all the enemy's plans
With Jesus Christ our Lord
So, rise up now and join me
In a Warrior Princess stance
Pray in our heavenly language
And defeat satan at first glance!

Watchmen, it is Time!

Watchmen, watchmen, God's calling you
There is no time to sleep
Take up your post upon the wall
Your city you must keep
From the plans of satan
Who wants to come right in
And sit right at our table
And tempt us into sin
Watchmen, watchmen, stand to attention
NOW it is YOUR TIME
God's recruiting in His army
He's saying – "YOU ARE MINE!"
To warn those all around you
Of pitfalls in this world
Satan's hoard of demons
Their debauchery is unfurled
Sin has infiltrated
In hearts that God wants pure
Satan tricks and he deceives
With his shiny lure
Watchmen, watchmen warn them all
For those who cannot see
Don't worry they think you're crazy
Push through until VICTORY!
In the realm of darkness
Oh yes – it's very real
Don't think that it is nothing
It is a very big deal
God has given you this gift
He wants not one to be lost
You MUST DECLARE the word of God
No matter what the cost
We must link arms and join together

In this united call
Gather those around you
It is for one and all
Watchmen, watchmen, now is your time
Pray on bended knee
Call them back from the darkness
DECLARE THEY ARE SET FREE!
And God will move upon your words
Shift strongholds with great power
Watchmen, watchmen, this is YOUR time
You were born for this very hour!

What is the Church?

What is Church all about?
I clearly hear you say
How is it relevant now
In our world today?
Bricks and mortar and full of rules
Religion creates wars
Why would I ever want
To enter through those doors?
Well, if you want to sit and hear
What I have to share
I'll tell you about my relationship
Then you can compare
That religion versus relationship
In a God who loves you so
Will answer your dilemma
And in your heart, you'll know
Why bricks and mortar are not the church
And men ruling the day
No – that is so far from it
God has set it up 'this' way
He sent His own son Jesus
To show the world His Love
And let Him die upon the cross
While He looked down from above
At you and me – God saw our hearts
And the state that we were in
Jesus came to die for us
To take away our sin
Then He rose again to Heaven
Way up in the sky
It's written in the Bible
God's word - it does not lie
Then the Holy Spirit came
To live in you and me

We just have to receive Him
And then you'll clearly see
That 'this' is the relationship
I am talking about
We are the church in this world
Yes! I can hear you shout!
You have been hurt by the church
Actually, I have too
Some people they have not behaved
Like God would want them to
And it gives God such a bad name
And creates a strong delusion
Religion wears the mask of love
But it's really just an illusion
Don't blame God for the powers of men
Doing their own thing
Their hardened hearts are full of pride
In their eyes, they are king
They've lost sight of the true plan
Of what religion is
It's relationship with Jesus
You simply are just His!
To love and share and really care
For others every day
God pours right down His beautiful love
To help you on your way
So, while you might not understand
What the church is really about
I hope my explanation
Will take away your doubt
And help you open up your heart
To a God who loves you so
My prayer for you is that one day
His love you'll come to know.

Why a Dark Church?

Why are some churches going dark?
And all I see is black
When I step inside one
They say it's a comfort hack
They tell me some people are just shy
And want to be left alone
Don't look at me and I won't look at you
I'll just sit here with my phone
To dim the lights for atmosphere
Well, that's another thing
That's actually quite soothing
When all our voices sing
But a church that's fully in the dark
What have you done this for?
It's really quite confusing
I can't even see the floor
This is not how God planned it
For when we come together
He wants us to embrace with love
Our arms around each other
That I can look straight into your eyes
And greet you with God's love
Our spirits together acknowledging
The Holy Spirit above
Entwining us together
Forging God's own plan
Not fumbling in the darkness
This is the work of man
God is light and He is truth
Shining bright with Glory
Please don't smother what God wants
Please show the Gospel story
The stage is lit, the fog is on

Am I at a concert?
This reminds me of my dark days
This atmosphere is no comfort
The devil delights in darkness
It's his way of covering sin
It's in God's light he is exposed
His counterfeit within
So don't be fooled in a dark church
Turn the lights on and really see
That it's God's light that brings the power
In light there's victory!
Forgive us God for blacking you out
It's like a golden calf
Men have built this idol
They think it's cool and laugh
But you don't think it's funny God
No No! – not at all
It's in the dark that people fail
It's easy for them to fall
So, shine your light back in the church
So, all the world can see
That it's only God's pure love and light
That heals and sets us FREE!

Why won't they Listen?

Lord, why won't they listen
To what I have to say?
Why do they shut me out
Day after day?
I share of your love
And your Heavenly peace
I tell them that their worries
With You shall all cease
They are not only deaf,
They are also blind
Even when I tell them
You are just SO kind
They cannot hear,
They cannot see
What a beautiful Saviour
To them YOU WILL BE!
Yet they live in the lie,
This world cares for them
BUT YOU are the TRUTH
And the God of ALL men
I pray that the veil
That covers their eyes,
Will be whisked away
And expose satan's lies
That keep them in chaos
With no peace in their heart
It's your DYING LOVE
That will bring a new start
And you'll love them forever
And walk by their side
Fill their life with your SPIRIT
And in them ABIDE

Together forever
NOW they hear and can see
What a BEAUTIFUL SAVIOUR
To them YOU WILL BE!

Will the Real Jesus please Stand Up!

Will 'THE REAL' Jesus please stand up!
And come and fill my spiritual cup
Fill me till I'm overflowing
So, I truly have that inner knowing
There is so much deception in the world
Satan's lies have been unfurled
White is black and black is white
Good is evil - it's just not right
Open your eyes, so you can see
The truth of Jesus so you will be free
His love is light and truth and grace
This love will make you see His face
And set you free with this Great Love
The Holy Spirit, the gentle dove
Will stamp on satan's lies and hate
Please do not take his twisted bait
He will lead you down a deep dark well
He calls it fun but it's really hell
Please don't go there - resist temptation
Because satan wants to destroy this nation
And pollute it with his death so vile
Every man and woman and every child
But Jesus is our only hope
To clear away satan's screens of smoke
And reveal his lies and stronghold snares
It's the living Jesus who truly cares
Open your mind and move your heart
Towards God's love and you'll be a part
Of God's true Kingdom – a city on a hill
But you need to be quiet, His voice is still

Come away with Jesus and His Great Love
He will whisper the secrets of Heaven above
That white is white and black is sin
No more lies will keep you trapped in
The darkness that this world dictates
Because the Bible now you can relate
It's guidance and justice and never-ending truth
Will train you to be a wise super sleuth
And see the real from the fake
No more garbage will you take
Because

THE REAL JESUS HAS STOOD UP

And overflowed your spiritual cup
Now full of Power and wisdom and grace
Your God-given birthright is your new race
Now go tell the world that Jesus is here
And His return is very near
To pour down His love into you and me
And take us all home to Eternity.

You are my Peace

In search for the truth in this mixed-up world
I called out for an answer
All the world said back was
You're unlucky your star signs a Cancer
Nightmare after nightmare
Living in despair and fear
Where do I get this PEACE from
I search for year after year
I was always told it was pot-luck
Which side of the coin one was born
There must be more to life than
Confusion, sickness, worry and scorn
I tried tobacco, grass and drink
Money, clothes and endless men
I must have missed something along the way
So, I tried them all again
One day a man came across my path
Who I thought was never real
YOU were 'just a name' but
JESUS, your presence I feel
"How could this be true", I spoke
You were just 'The Christmas Tale'
Then as 'the truth' appeared to me
My heart began to wail
"Be like a child", Jesus said to me
"Never try to work me out,
Just TRUST My Father's written word
And you shall never doubt
I have come to save you
And hold you in my arms
I AM your PEACE and power
Throw away your lucky charms

I will live on earth with you
Just ask me in your heart
Wipe away those childhood tears
I'll give you a brand-new start
And when your life has ended here
Your breath will heave a sigh
I will come and take your spirit
To Heaven, you and I"

"All these things you've said to me
I find so hard to conceive
But like a child
You said, I only have to believe
I can't deny the joy you give me
I can't deny your love
I can't deny the Holy Spirit
So gentle as a dove"
That frantic search is finally over
My old life now does cease
YOU made my spirit born-again
JESUS...YOU ARE MY PEACE.

You are our Legacy

I know you, God, because you knew me
Before I was even formed
You grew me in my mother's womb
Where my features were adorned
With my unique beauty
Fashioned from your hand
You love me more than I'll ever know
But I'll try to understand
That you wrote for me a blueprint
To discover in my life
And you planned for me a future
Full of good things and not strife
Every year that I did grow
And every step I took
Your unfailing love surrounded me
You touched my eyes to look
To find your son called Jesus
And see Him on the cross
T'was MY sin that kept us separate
But Jesus, you took my loss
And gave to me an open door
For me to walk right through
Jesus made the way, Father
For me to come back to you
The Creator of my being
You are my ABBA God
And those who don't understand this
Just think that I am odd
But I'll declare your love for me
And stand upon your word
I'll share your truth, your way, your life
And I'll make sure I am heard

To spread your message far and wide
Of your love that sets us free
Because we are your children
And YOU ARE our Legacy!

Your Hope

What makes you so different Christian
In this world today?
Because darkness is getting darker
In every possible way
Well, I'm so very glad you asked
I have one thing to show
That in this world I'm not alone
For My Saviour, I do know
Jesus, He stands by my side
And gives to me His light
So, in this world that's oh so dark
I can shine so bright
And that's not all Jesus gives to me
His love, His peace, His joy
All these things are a weapon of strength
I have them to employ
Not just for me but for others too
Who need love in their day
All they have to do is receive
To live the Jesus way
And darkness, fear and all things bad
Will do no harm at all
Because God will pursue them with His love
And they will hear Him call
Their very name so loud and clear
And make no blind mistake
That all who call to Jesus
He will not forsake
So, my friend as the world grows dim
And your days are hard to cope
Look to the brightness of the Lord
AND HE WILL BE YOUR HOPE!

Your Love Never Ends

Jesus, you are my very best friend
Your love for me has no end
Your love for me is like no other
Even deeper, than a mother
You've seen me laugh
You've seen me cry
And you understand
The reasons why
You catch every tear
You know every fear
And every day
Your love does stay
Holding me close in your arms
And always safe from satan's harms
You have a plan for where I must go
Even when it seems so slow
But as I wait and pray and BE
Eventually – in time I see
That you have kept the very best
And all I had to do was rest
In your perfect love that has no end
Jesus, you are my very best friend.

Connect with Megan

I would love to hear from you through;

 www.heartweaves.com

 heartweaversinc@gmail.com

 Facebook: Megan Reda

Write to me

HEARTWEAVES
PO BOX 1440
MANDURAH WA 6210

My Child and the Tapestry of Life

All the proceeds fund our on-site
TRAUMA HEALING WORKSHOPS

Purchase My Child and the Tapestry of Life
in softcover from the website shop
@ www.heartweaves.com

Download FREE PDF Trauma Healing worksheets
@ www.heartweaves.com

www.ingramcontent.com/pod-product-compliance
Lightning Source LLC
Chambersburg PA
CBHW062048290426
44109CB00027B/2768